carpets

for the home

carpets

for the home

Amicia de Moubray

and David Black

Laurence King

half-title: Carpet by Judy Ross for Salon Moderne, New York, used as a wall hanging in a Manhattan loft.

frontispiece: 'Richard Sackville, Third Earl of Dorset' (detail), by William Larkin.

below: The magnificent, typically wide border of a Ziegler Feraghan carpet from Persia, c.1860.

Published in 1999 by Laurence King Publishing
an imprint of Calmann & King Ltd
71 Great Russell Street, London WC1B 3BN
Tel + 44 171 831 6351 Fax + 44 171 831 8356 e-mail: enquiries@calmann-king.co.uk
www.laurence-king.com

ISBN 1 85699 130 6

A catalogue record for this book is available from the British Library

Designed by Michael Tighe. Special photography by Christopher Simon Sykes, Andrew Wood, John Hall and Angelo Hornak. Location research by Amicia de Moubray and David Black. Specialist advice by Jennifer Wearden and Adam Chadwick. Picture research by Nadine Bazar, Mary-Jane Gibson and David Black. Cartography by Ailsa Heritage and James Anderson.
Index by Helen Baz.

Printed in China

contents

introduction

Carpets – be they oriental or western in origin – are a fascinating subject and one that is highly rewarding to study. Despite their widespread use there is an aura of mystique about them. For most people buying a carpet is much more daunting than buying a sofa or a dining-room table. The reasons for this are manifold, the two main ones being the sheer quantity of the different types of western and oriental carpets available compounded by the fact that nearly all the major centres of oriental carpet production are in far-flung parts of the world, known only to carpet specialists. Apart from a few scholarly tomes, surprisingly little has been written about carpets that is readily accessible to the layman. The aim of this book is to reveal the extent of the exciting variety of western and oriental carpets most frequently encountered and to show how they can be used to great effect in a diverse range of interiors, historic or contemporary, urban or rural, all over the world.

The widespread use of carpets in the home is one of the most neglected aspects of the history of interior decoration in Europe and America. Perhaps it is their ubiquity that explains the scant attention they receive. We take them for granted. Look at any decorating magazine and carpets are lucky to get a one-line mention if at all. Compared with the inches of text and lavish photographs devoted to the latest furnishing fabrics, carpets, even highly prized oriental examples, are woefully ignored. This makes the task of choosing a carpet all the more difficult. Should one buy a flatweave, or a pile rug, something machine- or hand-woven, oriental or French? The choice can be baffling so it is not surprising that many people eventually choose the safe option of a wall-to-wall fitted carpet.

Yet carpets can bring so much to any room, whatever the size and whatever the style. A judiciously chosen carpet is a wonderful way of bringing together all the disparate elements of a room's decoration by echoing the prominent colours. Alternatively, a fabulous carpet can be used as a starting point for the decoration of a room, and the curtains, upholstery fabrics and so on can be chosen to complement the carpet. Typically the poor carpet is the last element of a room to be considered. This is a pity. If more thought was given at the outset of decorating a room the chances are that the carpet would be a stronger feature. And deservedly so. Carpets, by their very nature, are extremely tactile and consequently an ideal way of adding a warm texture to a room – whether as a floor covering or a wall hanging.

This book attempts to provide easy to follow guidelines for the reader who wants to know what kind of carpet would be suitable for their home, whether it is an elegant town house or an urban apartment, a rambling country farmhouse or a minimalist modern loft conversion. Given the huge scope it is impossible to discuss every type of carpet available so this book concentrates on the most readily accessible types of oriental and western carpets, both antique and contemporary. A succinct history of the production as well as the main characteristics such as motifs and colour palettes are outlined.

The price range of carpets is vast, and it is always difficult to specify the exact price one should pay for a particular type of carpet, as the market for carpets can be volatile. This can be explained by several factors, primarily the rarity, the quality of materials and weaving of the carpet, and its aesthetic value in the opinion of the carpet dealers and interior decorators. It is often the interior decorators who are instrumental in setting the market prices. For example, following the recent embargo on importing Persian carpets into America, canny Manhattan interior decorators were quick to promote French Aubussons as *the* carpets to have and consequently their price shot up and they became extremely sought after. The text offers general guidelines on the current pricing of carpets.

Recent years have witnessed a renaissance of carpet weaving using traditional patterns and natural dyes in traditional centres of carpet production, such as Turkey, so that it is now possible to have relatively inexpensive copies of antique carpets made. Inevitably as antique carpets become increasingly difficult to obtain more and more people will be commissioning replicas. Another recent trend has been a growing interest in contemporary designs made using traditional methods in historic centres of weaving.

Today the majority of homes contain at least one if not several carpets or rugs whether machine-made or hand-woven, flatwoven or knotted, western or oriental in origin, natural or chemical dyed, geometric or floral in design. The terminology carpet or rug can

Fragments of a Savonnerie carpet border sewn together at the Hotel Mansart in Paris, decorated by Jacques Garcia.

be confusing, suffice it to say that in the trade a carpet must be at least 6′ x 9′, anything smaller should be classified as a rug. However, in America the word rug is used more broadly to describe carpets of all shapes and sizes.

In the West we are surrounded by a multitude of colours and textures in our daily lives. It is instructive to look at a carpet and try to imagine the type of conditions in which it was made. Often the context in which carpets are seen in the West belie their humble origins, which range from carpets woven by tent dwellers to those made in tiny village workshops. Many a Park Avenue apartment or English stately home boasts fine carpets emanating from far-flung parts of the world and made by craftsmen in very basic surroundings. We seem to have taken the assimilation of oriental carpets into the western interior without for a moment questioning the seemingly cultural incongruity of a sofa upholstered in an English chintz standing on a Heriz carpet in a remote baronial Scottish castle. Or a Tibetan meditation mat in a ski lodge in Aspen, Colorado.

The photographs of beautiful interiors from all over the world, many of which were specially commissioned for this book, are a rich source of inspiration for the reader seeking illumination on what type of carpet to buy. They form a section of the book which is divided into clearly defined categories: the decorated look; rustic; traditional; staircases, halls and passages; ethnic; and contemporary. All the interiors have been chosen as outstanding examples of successful decorative schemes that without a doubt have been greatly enhanced by the inclusion of at least one if not several carpets, some contemporary, some antique. Each category fully explores the possibilities, taking into account the durability and the appearance of the different carpets shown. It takes time to build up one's confidence as to what carpet to choose, but these pictures should provide a host of ideas.

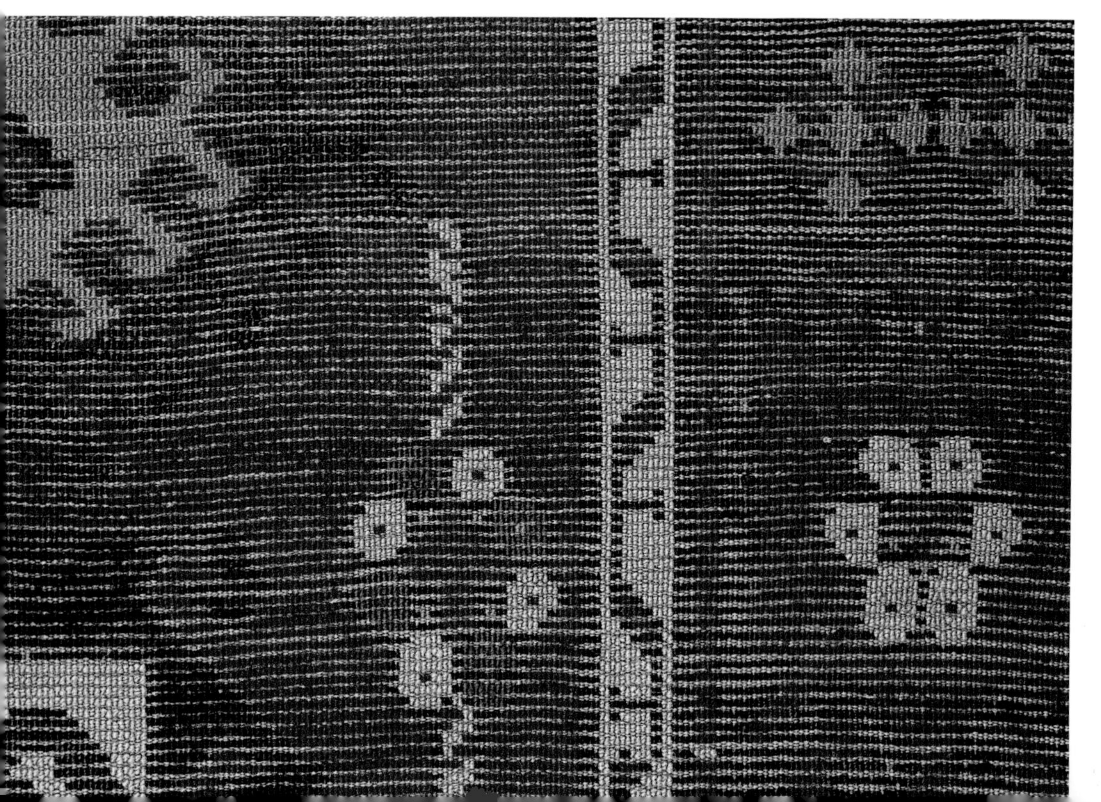

opposite: Detail of a Caucasian rug showing the reverse side. Late nineteenth century.

right: South Persian rug (detail) made by the Qashqai tribe. Lions and many other animals can be seen in the endless field. Late nineteenth century.

overleaf: A finely woven Tabriz carpet, c.1900, greatly enchances the formal entrance hall in a house in Australia.

The book ends with a mine of practical information including advice on the care and repair of carpets, a glossary of technical terms, an international directory of specialist carpet and rug dealers, a list of public collections of carpets to visit and suggested further reading. This has been put together with the invaluable help of leading international carpet specialists and scholars.

Once again there seems to be a burgeoning interest in carpets and the ancient skills associated with carpets are being revived just in time to prevent them being lost for ever. As this book sets out to demonstrate the world of carpets is marvellously rich and varied in its scope and its study is highly rewarding for anyone with an interest in the decorative arts. Carpets do much to enrich our surroundings and it is hoped that this book will awaken interest in an exciting field.

carpets in interiors: a history

Today carpets are an integral component of western domestic interiors. But it was not always so: until the mid-eighteenth century, the ownership of carpets in Europe was confined to royalty and the aristocracy. Gradually carpets became more widespread, but it was only in the wake of the industrial revolution that carpets became relatively inexpensive and therefore widely available for the first time. The history of the import of oriental carpets and their use in the western interior is a fascinating story of the important influence the trading routes of the great mercantile nations of the sixteenth, seventeenth and eighteenth centuries had on the decorative arts of the time and the evolution of interior decorating fashions.

The trade in oriental carpets to the West

Oriental carpets were probably the first pile carpets to be used in European and American interiors, and were brought back by crusaders and merchants from their travels in the Orient from the turn of the eleventh century. The ownership of an oriental carpet rapidly became a status symbol for royalty, members of the European aristocracy and other eminent figures, who had their portraits painted showing them standing proudly on finely depicted oriental carpets. They obtained the carpets by various means, either as diplomatic gifts or through merchants. For example, Cardinal Wolsey was given 60 carpets by a Venetian envoy in 1520 in return for his support in obtaining the repeal of the duties on wines from Candia (the Italian name for Crete), which Venetian traders imported into England. They were probably made in Egypt or in what is modern-day Syria. When Wolsey was dismissed as chancellor in 1529, all his goods, including his carpets, were forfeited to King Henry VIII.

'Marian Flowerpiece', c.1485, by Hans Memling. This is the earliest known still-life painting to contain a carpet as a major element of the composition.The carpet may be Turkish, but its coarse weave suggests it is more likely to be a Flemish-made copy based on imported Turkish carpets.

Carpets were used both as floor coverings and draped across tables in the manner of tablecloths in this early period, as depicted in many sixteenth- and seventeenth-century European paintings. An interesting outcome of the depiction of particular oriental carpets by leading European artists of the day, primarily Hans Holbein, Lorenzo Lotto and Hans Memling, is the subsequent nomenclature of the carpets after the artists themselves. Thus, 'Lotto' carpets were Turkish, and were depicted in European paintings by different painters, not just Lotto, from the 1520s until the late seventeenth century (see William Larkin painting overleaf). They are characterised by a rather rigid arabesque grid,

IHS

most frequently yellow on red. 'Holbein' carpets were also from Turkey, and were brightly coloured with a design that is characterised by a composition of large square panels of octagons, which in turn enclose an assortment of geometric motifs and stylised animal and bird forms. Holbein's famous double portrait 'The Ambassadors', in the collection of the National Gallery, London, depicts an excellent example of such a carpet. 'Memling' carpets are divided into square or rectangular compartments, each of which contains a hooked cross. The Hans Memling painting on the previous page shows a carpet in the 'Memling' carpet style, which is in fact a locally produced copy. Memling carpets were Turkish: although a hooked cross appears on much later Caucasian carpets, there is no relation between these and the sixteenth-century Memlings.

By the seventeenth century, an age of great prosperity and ever-expanding overseas trade for many European nations led to a thriving import business in oriental carpets to many European countries. The British East India Company was founded in 1600 under a charter from Queen Elizabeth I to establish trade by sea with Asia, as the Portuguese had already done. The first mention of carpets in company records appears in a letter dated 1611 in which one agent tells another that he is expecting delivery of their 'Turkey carpets', apparently as personal rather than company property. At that time the term 'Turkey' was used to describe any kind of oriental carpet, although they also came from Persia, the Caucasus and elsewhere in the Near East. The Dutch East India Company was established in 1602, and the French Compaigne des Indes in 1664. Propitiously it was a period that coincided with the apogee of the Persian carpet industry. Under the Safavid dynasty (1501–1736) in Persia the standard of carpet production was superb, and it is not surprising that many of them were to find their way into the great aristocratic power houses of Europe. As oriental carpets were still very expensive to buy in the West, cheaper and inferior copies of oriental designs, often woven with much larger knots and therefore coarser in design, were regularly made locally, as in the still-life painting illustrated on this page.

The increasingly widespread availability of imported eastern carpets by the eighteenth century meant that they were no longer the exclusive preserve of the upper classes. They became common in the households of the landed gentry, where they were customarily used in parlours and dining-rooms. Carpets were bought from specialist dealers and were also sold at public auctions.

The burgeoning European carpet industries that emerged during the eighteenth century resulted in the gradual tailing-off of interest in oriental carpets. Between 1770 and 1850 it is difficult to find Turkish or Persian carpets in contemporary depictions of fashionable European interiors. By the early nineteenth century, machine-woven European carpets were to be seen everywhere. oriental carpets were not to become fashionable again until the 1860s, when there was a revival of interest, partly due to their prominent display at the Great Exhibition of 1851 in London, which helped to reawaken the

public's interest throughout Europe.

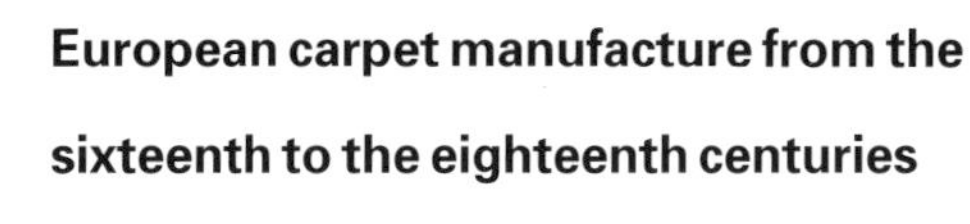

European carpet manufacture from the sixteenth to the eighteenth centuries

One of the earliest clear references to the existence of European carpet manufacture is in 1255, when Eleanor of Castile ostentatiously spread Spanish carpets upon the floor of her lodgings in Westminster before her marriage to Edward I of England. Spain was the first European country to establish a carpet-weaving industry following its invasion by the Moors in the early eighth century.

It was not until the sixteenth century in England and the early seventeenth century in France that

opposite: Mary Curzon, attributed to William Larkin (1580–1619), painted in 1612, the year of her marriage to Edward Sackville. The carpet is Turkish and known as a 'Lotto' after the painter Lorenzo Lotto, who included such carpets in his portraits. They typically feature an arabesque grid in yellow on a red ground.

below: Still life with nautilus cup, paten, ewers and gilt disk on a carpet draped over a ledge, circle of Francesco Fieravino, fl. 1650–80. The carpet shows a Turkish design influence, but some of the floral motifs and the coarseness of the knots suggest that it may be a cheaper Italian adaptation of a Turkish carpet.

other European countries followed suit in establishing their own carpet-weaving industries.The first knotted carpets made in Britain hailed from Ireland, and were made in imitation of the oriental style. The Earl of Ormonde and Ossory set up a group of Flemish weavers on his estate in County Kilkenny around 1512. The workshop was short-lived but it is an interesting example of aristocratic patronage attempting to establish a new craft industry. Later in the century there are a couple of recorded instances of entrepreneurs going to Persia intent on bringing back the secrets of the art of carpet making to Britain. In 1579 the geographer and author Richard Hakluyt (c.1522–1616) tried to entice back from Persia 'A singular good workeman in the arte of Turkish carpet making'. Sadly history does not relate if he was successful in his aim.

'Mr and Mrs Richard Bull' (detail),1747, by Arthur Devis (1712–1787). The rug is Turkish and was typical of the large rectangular carpets used in English country houses in the mid-eighteenth century at a time when oriental carpets were still fashionable. It appears to be a relatively coarsely knotted carpet. Many such carpets were exported via the port of Smyrna (modern Izmir) in Turkey and they are sometimes known as Smyrna carpets.

By the mid-eighteenth century in England two types of machine-woven English carpets were in greater demand than oriental carpets: Brussells (loop-pile) carpets; and Wilton (cut-pile) carpets. The technical advances behind this trend meant that, for the first time, carpets could be produced relatively inexpensively, quickly and, perhaps most importantly, could be tailor-made to fit a room. These carpets were produced in greater quantities in Britain than anywhere else, and were exported from Britain to America and elsewhere in Europe. They were also woven in other countries, including the Low Countries, France, and New Hampshire in America.

The mid-eighteenth century also saw knotted-pile carpets once again being woven in Britain. One of the leading manufacturers was Thomas Moore (c.1700–1788) 'Manufacturer and Hosier' of Chiswell Street, Moorfield, London, who boldly claimed on

his trade card to be 'The first in England, engaged in making the Royal Velvet Tapestry [that is, knotted pile] after the manner of the Persians'. By 1763 he had received the Royal Warrant and was described in 'The Universal Director' as having brought his 'Manufactory of English carpets to such perfection, that it far excels the Persians'. He is an important figure in the history of English carpets as he was responsible for weaving many of Robert Adam's great neo-classically inspired carpet designs. Adam's other carpets were hand-knotted in Axminster, Devon, at Thomas Witty's (1713–1792) carpet factory, started after he saw Turkish carpets in London in 1754.

Louis XV period room, 1735–40, 'Boiseries Rothschild', now in the Jerusalem Museum. This panelled room was originally in a Parisian house designed by Gabriel Boffrand for the banker Jacques-Samuel Bernard. The eighteenth-century Savonnerie carpet displays a wonderful contrast of light and dark colours.

overleaf: An elegant late eighteenth-century Axminster neo-classical carpet, probably originally made for Devonshire House, London. It is now in the Blue Drawing Room, in the private wing of Chatsworth House, Derbyshire, seat of the Duke of Devonshire.

The seventeenth and eighteenth centuries saw the establishment of a French carpet industry. Unlike the British or American carpet industries, the French were unique in that, instead of trying to emulate oriental carpets from the very beginning of their carpet production, they instigated their own designs. These typically comprised floral motifs intertwined with architectural motifs and scrolls and arabesques. Aubusson, best known for its tapestry-woven carpets, was established in 1742 and Savonnerie, producer of knotted-pile carpets founded by Louis XIII in 1627, were the two principal centres.

Savonnerie production was originally exclusively for the court. Aubusson carpets were sold originally to the French aristocracy, but became widely popular and available after about the 1820s. At that time, the Savonnerie and Aubusson carpets reflected the neo-classical Empire style in their design motifs, employing classical ornaments, although their floral motifs continued as a strong underlying theme throughout the companies' centuries of production.

SMITHFIELD

The arrival of carpets in America

There are close parallels in the early histories of the importation of oriental carpets to America and Europe. The crucial difference is that America was about a hundred years behind Europe, explained in part by the sheer distance of America from the Orient and also by the fact that the colonists were forbidden to trade directly with the East, which meant that all carpets had to be imported via Europe.

Spectacular Medallion Ushak carpets woven in Turkey, highly popular in Europe in the seventeenth century, were almost certainly among the first examples of oriental carpets to arrive in America in the eighteenth century, although early documentary evidence of this is scanty.

It was not until after the Revolution that America was able to set up its own carpet industry. The Whitty family, who made carpets for Robert Adam in Britain, were equally successful across the Atlantic. William Sprague, the son-in-law of Samuel Whitty who worked for the British branch, established a business in Philadelphia in the early 1790s making 'Turkey and Axminster' carpets, no doubt similar to those of his father-in-law. British manufactured carpets were greatly in demand in America for nearly one hundred and fifty years, from the middle of the eighteenth century until the end of the nineteenth century, by which time the heavy tariffs imposed by the government in the 1890s against the importation of British carpets led to their final demise. By that time, American connoisseurs had become more interested in importing oriental carpets. Important American collectors of oriental carpets of the period included J.P. Morgan, Henry Frick and Benjamin Altman, all of whom gathered together collections of superlative oriental carpets.

The long tradition of wealthy cosmopolitan Americans making trips to Europe to buy fashionable decorative accessories to adorn their homes may possibly have originated with affluent eighteenth-century Americans purchasing oriental carpets or British carpets in London, either making the trip themselves or buying through a London agent. For instance when Benjamin Franklin was in London in 1765 he bought 'A large Turkey carpet cost 10 Guineas for the Dining Parlour'.

'The Daughters of Edward D. Boit', 1882, by John Singer Sargent (1856–1925). The carpet is either American or British and is in keeping with the 'Aesthetic' style of the interior depicted.

From the nineteenth century to the present day

The rapid technological advances following the industrial revolution revolutionised the carpet industries all over Europe and America. For the first time ever carpets were no longer the exclusive reserve of the affluent classes. However the standard of designs being produced swiftly began to deteriorate as the manufacturers endeavoured to appeal to the common denominator of taste. The burgeoning middle classes were eager to furnish their new homes with the latest style of relatively inexpensive carpets. Charles Eastlake, the British author of the seminal work 'Hints on Household Taste' wrote in 1868, 'If people will prefer a bouquet of flowers or a group of spaniels worked upon their hearth-rug...it is difficult to convince them of their error'.

'A Moment's Rest', c.1880, by Denis Pierre Bergeret. A French interior showing two Caucasian carpets laid end-to-end in front of the fireplace, on top of what could be a machine-woven European carpet. The painting illustrates the popularity of oriental carpets in Europe at the time.

A growing band of vociferous critics began to raise their objections to the poor standards of design prevalent and increasingly turned back to oriental carpets, which led to a renaissance of interest in oriental carpets in Europe in the 1860s and 1870s, when the possession of one became de rigueur for any fashionable interior.

The last quarter of the nineteenth century was a period of great change in the history of taste in carpets and one whose influence continues to the present day. A pivotal figure was the British artist and designer William Morris (1834–1896), who was probably the first to produce 'Designer Rugs' with his Arts and Crafts carpets. Extremely knowledgeable, Morris himself collected oriental carpets and was responsible for important museum acquisitions of carpets in America and Britain. It is thanks to Morris advising the American donor, Frederick L. Ames, that the Boston Museum of Fine Art owns one of the most celebrated Mughal rugs in existence, woven in Lahore c.1590–1600.

It is probably fair to say that the beginning of modern carpet design can be dated to 1880, when Morris & Co. mounted an

German school , c.1835, interior of a drawing room with a view into a garden. The carpet is European, possibly English, and must have been new when painted because similar designs are dated to the 1830s.

exhibition in its Oxford Street shop in London of an impressively wide range of Morris Arts and Crafts rugs and carpets accompanied by a leaflet saying, 'It is an attempt to make England independent of the East for the supply of hand-made carpets which may claim to be considered works of art...We people of the West must make our own hand-made carpets...and these, while they should equal the Eastern ones as nearly as may be in materials and durability, should by no means imitate them in design, but show themselves obviously to be the outcome of modern and Western ideas, guided by those principles that underlie all architectural art in common'.

In addition to Morris's hand-woven carpets, he was also responsible for a range of designs for machine-woven carpets which were available and popular on both sides of the Atlantic. Morris & Co. carpets were available at Bumstead & Co. and Goldthwaite & Co. in Boston. An American critic, writing in the publication 'Art Interchange' in 1879, had high praise for Morris: 'In Morris's hands the despised Kidderminster [a machine-woven flatweave carpet] which up to that time was used only for bedrooms or housekeepers' rooms, became a thing of beauty'. Today, Morris carpets are highly sought after and consequently command enormous prices.

The Arts and Crafts movement led to a few carpet manufacturers producing hand-knotted carpets in that style. The most important was the English firm Alexander Morton & Co., who enlisted C.F.A. Voysey (1857–1941), a leading figure in the English Arts and Crafts movement, to design ten carpets a year, initially for five years, beginning in 1897. Morton & Co. also set up a carpet workshop in Killybegs, a small fishing village in a remote stretch of coast in County Donegal, Ireland. Donegal carpets were sold in America by Gustav Stickley, a leading figure in the American Arts and Crafts movement at his 'Craftsman' showrooms in New York.

The beginning of the twentieth century was overshadowed by the First World War and it is not until the 1920s that carpets are once again worth examining, the sole exception being the carpets produced by the Omega Workshop. This was a short-lived enterprise set up in England in 1913 by the art critic Roger Fry to improve decorative design in England, enlisting designers such as Duncan Grant, Vanessa Bell and Henri Gaudier-Brezska. The carpets are highly daring in their use of colour and bold patterns. They were hand-knotted by the Wilton Royal Carpet Factory.

The popular International Exhibition of Modern Decorative and Industrial Art in Paris in 1925 was to have a huge impact on carpet design throughout Europe and America. The stylistic term 'Art Deco' arose from the exhibition, which in retrospect can be seen to be a statement of France's supremacy in the decorative arts. The traditions of luxury and supreme quality of workmanship were exemplified in all areas of the interior by virtue of decorators such as Jacques-Emile Ruhlmann (1879–1933), who was responsible for the organisation of the centrepiece in the exhibition, the 'Hotel du Collectionneur' (see illustration on page 28). The immense carpet in this interior, commissioned by Ruhlmann and designed by Emile Gaudissard, combines clean, definitive lines with stylised floral patterning in shades of rose and blue. It is a wonderful example of the

The 'Fintona' carpet at The Deanery, Berkshire, England. This Donegal carpet, woven for Liberty of London c.1902, was possibly designed by the Silver Studio, a workshop set up by Arthur Silver (1853–96) to design a wide range of products in many different media.

style of carpets produced both for and by Ruhlmann. Yet it was those carpets that owed less to tradition, which were also included in the exhibition and were inspired by the avant-garde French painters such as the Cubists, that were to become increasingly popular in the late 1920s and 1930s. The designer Ivan da Silva Bruhns, who collaborated with the firm of Jules Leuleu from 1924, was at the forefront of this field. His carpet for the Maharaja of Indore at the Manik Bagh Palace in 1930 is just such an example (see illustration on facing page), which combines a subtlety of tone and shade with strong graphic colour blocks and often whimsical patterns. His conviction and commitment to the importance of carpet design led to his insistence that an interior be adapted to his work, rather than the reverse.

By the 1930s, the artist-designed carpet had become a recognised commodity in its own right, exploiting the increased emphasis given to textiles in modern interiors, which were

The grand salon in the Hotel du Collectionneur at the 1925 International Exhibition of Modern Decorative and Industrial Art in Paris, decorated and furnished by Jacques-Emile Ruhlmann. Ruhlmann commissioned the immense carpet, which combines a strong linear design with floral patterns in shades of rose and blue, from the designer Emile Gaudissard.

Geometric carpet, 3.35 x 6.4m (10′ x 20′3″), designed by Ivan da Silva Bruhns for the Maharaja of Indore at the Manik Bagh Palace, c.1930.

characterised by the interplay of space and light. Following da Silva Bruhns's lead, more designers concentrated solely on such design, and the American Marion Dorn's (1896–1964) sobriquet 'the architect of floors' neatly encapsulates this new outlook.

Dorn designed over one hundred carpets including commissions for London's Savoy and Berkeley Hotels and Syrie Maugham's daring 'all-white' drawing room in 1931. Many of her rugs were woven by specialist departments within established carpet firms such as Wilton Royal, Axminster and Edinburgh Weavers, yet she was astute enough to realise the value of promoting her carpets in limited editions of only six or seven.

Immediately after the Second World War, the age of the designer carpet seemed to have disappeared for ever. But happily, recent years have witnessed a resurgence of interest in carpets which has led to their revival, a century after William Morris's efforts at improving carpet design and production. It is also a century since the last so-called 'revival period' took place in the traditional centres of weaving in the Orient. Once again carpets are being woven for the western market in the East, more often than not to contemporary designs, although there is also growing demand for accurate and readily affordable reproductions of historic designs, such as Indian Agra carpets or French Aubussons, which are now beyond the budget of all but the serious collector. This recent growing recognition amongst interior decorators of the important contribution that a beautiful carpet can make to an interior means that this is an exciting time to invest in contemporary carpets.

carpets in interiors

a rich source of inspiration from around the world

the decorated look

'We have passed from the golden age of architecture to the gilded age of decoration' wrote Edith Wharton in 1897 announcing a new phenomenon – the interior decorator.

A hundred years later, interior decorators are more in demand than ever. There has been an explosion of interest in what is now regarded as a proper industry. It is a field led by the Americans who have long turned to professionals to advise on what look is of the moment, with the British and French following closely behind.

For carpet dealers and the various auction house specialists, decorators, particularly New York luminaries, are an extremely powerful sector of the market. Decorators can easily influence fashions, dictating a style of carpet that overnight becomes de rigueur. An example is the recent rise in popularity of nineteenth-century Aubussons. Many a home on New York's fashionable Upper East side boasts a drawing room or bedroom featuring floral patterned Aubusson carpets in rose-coloured palettes. This fashion was entirely promoted by a few decorators anxious to find a substitute for Persian carpets because of the US embargo on importing goods from Iran as a result of the 1979 revolution. As in all areas of style consciousness, decorators are known for their particular look and often choose a similar type of carpet. It can be instructive to see what type of carpet someone with such a honed eye chooses. The confidence and years of looking, that is all part of the trade, means that often what at first might seem a surprising choice of carpet or rug is in reality very successful.

Many decorators are now taking advantage of the revival of interest in traditional methods of carpet production and commissioning individual designs for their clients whether it be for a contemporary style interior or for a more sober traditional look. It must be very exciting to have a client open to new ideas and prepared to commission a new carpet, an option that is not as prohibitively expensive as it sounds, and in fact very often cheaper than buying an antique example. It is a particularly good solution for large rooms.

The interiors in this chapter show the enormous range of options that the decorated look can embody.

previous pages: 'Master and his wife', c.1523, painted by Lorenzo Lotto (c.1480–1556) – a Lotto carpet is used to cover the table.
right: A superb Caucasian carpet in a Lori-Pambak design with vegetable dyes sits well in the style writer Suzanne Slesin's New York apartment.

left top: A 1920s Turkish kilim in a London drawing room provides a good background for an unusual collection of decorative objects.
left, second from top: The pretty colours of this cotton flatweave add to the light, airy feeling of this American attic bedroom.
left, third from top: A fine Luristan kilim, c.1870, is used to great effect decoratively draped over a table in the London kitchen of Emma Burns, a designer with Sybil Colefax, the decorating division of Colefax & Fowler.
left bottom: A nineteenth-century cabbage rose design carpet in Valentino's London house decorated by Colefax & Fowler.
right: A superb Feraghan carpet, c.1860, with an unusually large palmette design helps to soften the palatial proportions of a London drawing room and is a strong element in the overall scheme. The brilliant colour palette is typical of Feraghan carpets.

above: A modern Afghan carpet adds a bold dash of pattern to an otherwise restrained American den.

right: Late nineteenth-century armchairs upholstered with pieces of machine-made carpets with oriental designs, in a Parisian apartment decorated by Jacques Grange. Chairs of this type were made by Shoolbred, Tottenham Court Road, London, c.1880.

above left: A zigzag carpet designed by John Stefanidis for his own country house in Dorset. The room is an excellent example of how a carpet can contribute to a colour scheme.

above right: A contemporary pile rug designed by Sandy Jones is proof that antiques and modern design can blend handsomely together in a London town house.

left: Another contemporary pile rug designed by Sandy Jones is an excellent example of how the imaginative use of just two colours can create a subtly powerful design for a carpet in the bedroom of a London town house.

opposite right: An artist designed carpet in a stylish Parisan interior designed by the French decorator, Jean-Louis Riccardi.

LAURE

ISTANBUL

A needlepoint carpet by Benita Kussel in a bedroom decorated by the antique dealer Marroun Salloum, echoes the design of the bed cover.

previous pages left: An elegant rug designed by Christopher Farr and hand-woven in Konya, central Turkey, blends effortlessly into a sophisticated coolly decorated bedroom in a London town house. *previous pages right:* A carpet designed by Judy Ross for Salon Moderne, New York, makes a dramatic statement in the dining-room of architect Alison Platt's Sagaponack farmhouse on Long Island, America. *this page right:* A modern reproduction of a Wiener Werkstatte carpet in the highly idiosyncratic drawing room of the London home of English textile designers Sue Timney and Grahame Fowler.

left top: An easy on the eye flatwoven cotton rug adds a degree of comfort to an American bathroom in a country house in Long Island. *below:* The graphic lines of a specially designed black and white carpet give this traditional room in Cyprus a contemporary feel. *right:* The library room in the London home of designers Sue Timney and Grahame Fowler. They designed the carpet specially themselves and it was hand-woven in Scotland. The bookshelves and the table are both made from reclaimed 100-year-old railway sleepers. The 1930s fireplace is from Liberty, London.

GILBERT & GEORGE
Blumenfeld

above: A flatweave cotton carpet in cream and blue echoes the overall colour scheme of a small guest bedroom at Elgahamar, Sweden. *right:* A pretty floral carpet is eminently suitable for the ultra-feminine look of a bedroom in the Normandy home of Lillian Williams, who is an enthusiast for eighteenth-century style French interiors.

left: A splendid huge Luristan kilim, c.1910, is used to great effect in a very sophisticated house in Greece.

right top: A late nineteenth-century Turkish kilim is used to bring colour and pattern to a rustic villa in Patmos in the Greek Islands.

right below: A surprising mix of French chairs and an Indian dhurrie work well together in a house in Majorca.

above: A mid-twentieth-century floral American rug adds an element of femininity to a guest bedroom in a Florida artist's home.

right: A Karabagh carpet, c.1930, the design of which inspired the perfume and soap packaging of the period, in an attic eyrie in Paris.

rustic

Of all the different styles of western interiors, it is perhaps the more rustic in feel that are the nearest in spirit to the indigenous environments of many oriental carpets. The basic interiors typical of early American homes are the forerunners of what, ever since the Arts and Crafts movement, has been a conscious vogue for interiors that delight in the simple life. It does not matter if they are skilfully contrived or genuine, it is a look that satisfies a nostalgic vision of a seemingly pure way of life as well as being a retreat from the daily rigours of frenetic modern living. Carpets and rugs sit particularly happily in such interiors, injecting a welcome dash of pattern and colour into rooms that are often predominantly decorated in earth tones.

As can be seen from the following pages, flatweaves of any kind lend themselves beautifully to simple interiors: oriental kilims, Navajo rugs or Indian dhurries. The Bloomsbury group were prime exponents of this look in many of their homes. Avant-garde in so many ways, the Bloomsbury's taste for Turkish kilims was way ahead of their time. Throughout the nineteenth century and even into the early twentieth century old kilims were used to wrap up bales of pile carpets being shipped from the Orient to the West, such was their lack of status. The decorative qualities of kilims were not properly recognised until the London Whitechapel Gallery's seminal exhibition 'The Undiscovered Kilim' in 1977. From that date on their popularity as affordable furnishing carpets has soared in the West.

The homespun qualities of American rag or hooked rugs are also eminently suitable, as are the striped cotton runners typical of nineteenth-century Swedish interiors, personified by Carl Larsson. English designer Roger Oates has been imaginative enough to recognise the timeless appeal of nineteenth-century Venetian flatweaves which were made throughout the British Isles and have no known connection with the Italian city. He has successfully re-coloured them to a palette suitable for contemporary taste.

It is probably easier to incorporate carpets harmoniously into the rustic interior than into sophisticated design-led rooms, which tend to have a number of highly decorative elements all competing for attention. The key is to experiment and see what works best for you.

An oval rag rug adds an element of pattern and colour to a hearth in a house in Orford, New Hampshire, very much in the spirit of early eighteenth-century American houses.

above: A rag rug in an attic nursery in a house in Deerfield, Massachusetts, New England, an historic town of mainly Federal-style houses open to the public.
right: An example of the Bloomsbury group's avant-garde taste is the use of a gegim, c.1860, in the sitting room at Charleston, East Sussex.

right: A kilim from central Turkey, c.1870, in the sitting-room at Leonard and Virginia Woolf's residence, Monk's House, East Sussex, now a National Trust property. Woven in two halves because of the confined space available to the weavers, the kilim was subsequently sewn together. The tables and chairs were painted by Vanessa Bell and Duncan Grant.

left top: A modern Turkish kilim on the floor and an embroidery from East Turkestan on the bed add warmth and colour to a bedroom in a chalet in France.

left below: The geometric design and bright colours of this small Persian flatweave lend this French rustic bathroom a sophisticated air.

LA MUERTE DE PICASSO

previous pages left: A happy example of textiles and carpets from several different countries used together to create a highly decorative interior. Turkish covering is used around the bath and the floor next to a fragment of an antique Afghan kilim in English potter Mary Wondrausch's country cottage. She made the tiles above the bath, which depict rare breeds of bantams. The slipware plates on the walls above are also by Wondrausch.
The judicious use of different carpets in a small attic room in Wondrausch's cottage *(previous pages right)* creates a rich visual ensemble: the bed is covered with a Qashqai rug that has a typically strong colour palette, c.1860, the floor is covered with a Turkoman flatweave carpet, and in the bottom left hand corner a glimpse of a Turkey carpet, c.1900, can be seen.
Another imaginative mix of different carpets and ethnic textiles in her sitting-room *(right)*. A Navajo blanket, c.1910, is used as a throw on the sofa, a Turkoman flatweave covers the right arm of the sofa, a kilim is used to cover the table on the right, a Turkish yastik hangs underneath the window, an antique Sind wedding shawl is used as a door curtain and hand-blocked indigo Transylvanian hemp curtains surround the window.

Esst und trinkt
So lang's Euch schmeckt
Schon mal ist uns
Geld verreckt.

opposite: A typical chemically dyed washed-out Turkish kilim, c.1910–20, adds a welcome note of pattern in a Norwegian country house. *right:* The use of a typical Swedish cotton runner in Carl and Karin Larsson's home, Lilla Hyttnas, in the Swedish village of Sundborn is an important element in what would otherwise seem a somewhat austere room. *below right:* Again, simple striped cotton runners greatly enhance the dining-room at Lilla Hyttnas.

previous pages: A Moroccan flatweave provides a striking background for French designer Gérard Rigot's witty animal furniture.
above: A simple flatwoven cotton checked rug in the classic colour combination of blue and white adds an element of comfort in a villa bedroom in Tuscany.
right: A contemporary flatwoven runner by Roger Oates is inspired by striped nineteenth-century Venetian carpets, commonly used on staircases, passages, lobbies and occasionally bedrooms in English country houses. Few original examples remain in situ.
opposite: A modern cotton rug adds warmth and texture to a summer house in a Dorset garden.

A typical large format Thracian kilim, c.1900, with the Tree of Life design, echoes the square format of a room in an American country house in Massachusetts. The predominant red colour obtained from cochineal is very characteristic of Thracian carpets.

traditional

Since the eighteenth century, carpets have, in one form or another, become an integral component of western interiors. Given the exotic origins of oriental carpets it is astonishing that they are the most conventional choice when it comes to traditional-style interiors in Europe and America.

As the illustrations in this chapter demonstrate, oriental carpets are surprisingly versatile and can be used with great success in traditional-style interiors ranging from kitchens to drawing rooms to bedrooms. Often the context in which carpets are seen in the West belie their humble origins. Many a Park Avenue apartment or an English stately home has fine carpets emanating from far-flung areas of the world and made by weavers in very basic surroundings. We appear to have taken the assimilation of oriental carpets into the West without ever questioning the seemingly cultural incongruity of a Joshaghan carpet used in a Swedish castle or a Qashqai kilim in an American country house.

All too often the choice of carpet for a room's decorative scheme is added as an afterthought. This is a shame as carpets can be used rather like a painting to bring a room to life and they can be an excellent way of adding warmth and colour to any interior setting. In many ways it makes sense to use a carpet as the starting point for a decorative scheme. Also, it can be very effective to use several different types of carpet in the same room (see page 77). It is surprising how well carpets which are produced hundreds of miles apart in the Orient, or even in different continents, can work together lying side by side. The myriad colours and patterns of the literally thousands of carpets available are a truly rich source of inspiration. Look carefully at the rooms illustrated in this chapter – they may not be avant-garde but they all have their own individual style in which the carpet is very much a key element.

A marvellous example of a Sparta carpet, an inexpensive type of carpet made in Turkey in the 1920s specifically for the western market, used to its full decorative effect.

It is a high time that the sixteenth- and seventeenth-century custom of using carpets to drape tables was more widespread (see page 78). Not only is it an easy way in which to bring a dash of opulence to a room, it is also an intelligent way of using a carpet that is slightly worn. Holes or unsightly patches of worn pile can easily be hidden with a judiciously placed ornament.

above, top: A fine example of an Axminster carpet, c. 1785, in the Yellow Drawing Room in the private wing of Chatsworth House.

below: A bedroom at Harewood House, Yorkshire, with an Aubusson carpet, c.1830, woven with a central floral medallion.

right: A chemically dyed Turkish village carpet, a type popular in England at the turn of the century in the drawing room of Fillongley Hall, near Coventry. The fine- detailed severely geometric pattern is typical. Relatively inexpensive today.

left top: An elegant Chinese carpet, c.1920, which has a design similar to that of great nineteenth-century Chinese rugs, in a London dining-room. The blue is typical of Chinese rugs, the use of pink is more unusual.

left middle: An imaginative use of a Chinese carpet, c.1930s, which shows a clearly discernible western Art Deco influence in a London kitchen.

left bottom: A rare example of a splendid Heriz carpet, c.1860–70. A marvellous light medallion design in the centre field and a strong dark blue border act as a natural frame to the card table and chairs at Sledmere, Yorkshire.

right: An assortment of oriental carpets with a wide range of patterns and colours in an informal sitting-room in a country house in Yorkshire. The carpet in the foreground is from north-west Persia, the main carpet is a Heriz and the carpet nearest the armchairs is Caucasian.

left: An example of how an inexpensive 1930s kilim can be used to great effect in a simple Swedish-style interior in designer Sasha Waddell's London town house.
above: A late nineteenth-century Luri kilim on the floor of a guest bedroom in an American country house in Connecticut.

left above: A good example of the type of chemically washed Persian carpets popular in the West in the 1920s is used here to decorative effect to cover a table in an English country house.

left below: A late nineteenth-century Heriz carpet in front of the sofa suits the casual elegance of this drawing-room decorated in the traditional English country house look.

right: A Turkish kilim, c.1920s, is an ideal complement to the other colours in this French bathroom in a house on the Isle de France.

above: The detailed design of a rich-textured Persian Bakhtiari carpet, c.1900, sits well in this library setting.

right: An Erivan rug made in the 1920s for the western market, in a Swedish house.

far right: A finely woven Shirvan rug from the Caucasian lowlands, c.1920, is a good example of a commercial production using chemical dyes in a house in Chelsea, London.

ALGARDI
ALGARDI

above: A Joshaghan carpet, c.1920, discreetly brings life into a sombre room at Tureholm Castle, Sweden.

right: Fashionable artistic interiors of the late nineteenth century often featured eastern and oriental pieces. Shown here is a corner of Leighton House in London with a fine Caucasian carpet, c.1880s, a type of carpet fashionable at the time.

1

previous pages left: A striking carpet of Empire design in the Lantern Room at Rosendal in Sweden, with painted decoration by Pehr Emanuel Limnell.

previous pages right: Fine example of a neo-classical carpet in a palace in Compiegne, France. The chairs are upholstered in silk from Lyons.

left above: Modern copy of a grand Savonnerie carpet in a fashion designer's home in Italy.

left below: The carpet was woven specially for this eighteenth-century palace in northern Italy at the time it was decorated.

right: A nineteenth-century Madrid white wool carpet with central motif, strewn with bouquets of flowers, decorates the library room of Château Groussay near Versailles, France. The room was designed by Emilio Terry. It was completed in 1942 and is said to have inspired Cecil Beaton's set for Professor Higgins's study in 'My Fair Lady'.

staircases, halls & passages

It is notoriously difficult to decide what type of carpet is most suitable for stairs, hallways and passages, as all are areas that take a heavy pounding of feet and therefore require robust carpets. An alternative is to commission a carpet designer to draw up a design. The result will be not only unique, but is also a welcome act of patronage both for the designer and for all those involved with the production, from the dyers to the weavers.

One's first impression of a house is created by the hallway, so it is important to choose particularly carefully when selecting a carpet or rug. Pile carpets, inherently resilient by their nature, are an obvious choice. In terms of practicality it is perhaps wise to opt for a carpet with a dark colour palette which is capable of absorbing a certain amount of dirt brought in from outside without it being immediately obvious.

An important consideration when choosing a carpet for a stairway is the function of the space acting as it does as a link between all the different parts of a house. Stair carpets perform a dual function, one to dampen the noise and secondly as an opportunity to add another element of colour or pattern to a building. The choice of carpet has to co-ordinate all the way from the ground floor up to the top. It is understandable that the majority of people opt for the simple but dull solution of a plain fitted staircase carpet for the sake of playing safe. But that is to miss an exciting opportunity for making a decorative statement. One imaginative and very successful solution to the problem of stairs is shown on pages 94 and 95, an ideal way in which to use the odd fragment of old carpets. An experienced carpet fitter should be capable of combining odd pieces of old runners together. (Note that it would be extremely expensive, not to mention highly irresponsible, if one were to use complete carpets and chop them up.) Another idea is to select a boldly patterned type of carpet such as the jolly brightly coloured modern kilim on page 95, which has been used to transform a narrow London staircase into a strong decorative statement.

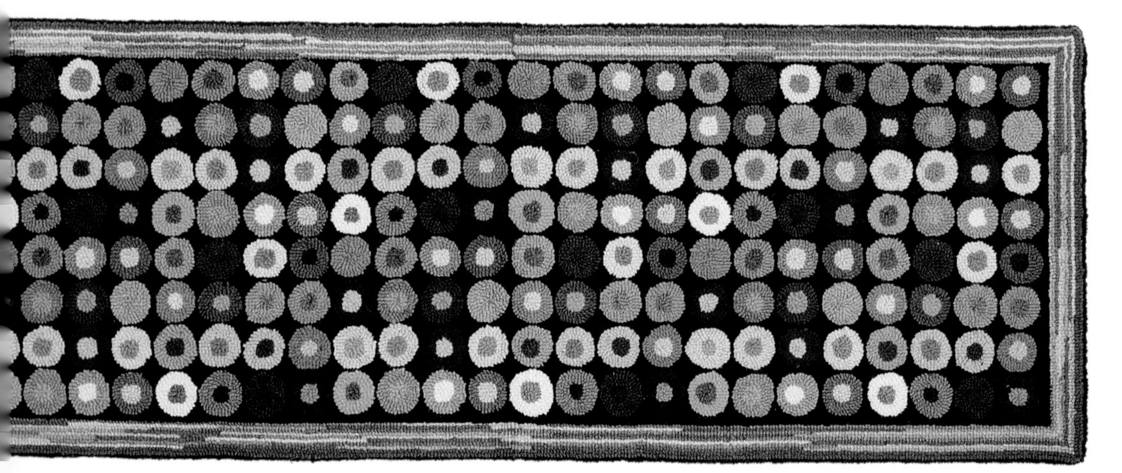

left: Hand-hooked runner with a design based on buttons by Claire Murray, a contemporary American designer based in Nantucket. *right:* Woven runner in a passageway in a house in Perigord, France.

previous pages left: The vertical stripes of a contemporary flatwoven runner designed by Roger Oates, are highly suitable for a stair carpet; *middle:* A contemporary stair carpet in a London town house, designed by Danielle Hartwright, woven in Egypt and inspired by an antique Ottoman design; *right:* Traditional handmade stair runner in Provincetown, New England, showing an idiosyncratic history of the area, from tepees and pilgrims to an artist by the sea.

left: An ingenious solution to a stair carpet is this bold combination of fragments of Caucasian and late nineteenth-century Turkish kilims laid to form a whole in an English country house.

above: Modern Turkish kilims are well suited to being used as stair carpets.

above: Oriental rugs and kilims are scattered around the hallway of this house in Portugal. This used to be the custom in Turkish mosques before the recent trend of replacing antique mosque carpets with modern machine-made reproductions became rife.

right: A carpet in Campbell tartan adds warmth to a staircase at Cawdor Castle, Inverness.

A Turkish Ushak kilim runner, c.1920, on the landing of a house in Gascony. When using a carpet like this, which is more decorative than practical, it is a good idea to use a non-slip underfelt which will strengthen it immeasurably.

above: A Kerman runner from south-west Persia probably made for the western market in the last quarter of the nineteenth century sits handsomely in the entrance hall of an English country house in Gloucestershire.

right: A very fine Caucasian runner, c.1860, with a typically rich colour palette, seen here in the entrance hall of a Dublin town house.

ethnic

It would be wrong to dismiss what today are called 'ethnic interiors' as a legacy of the hippy era. In fact they have a distinguished pedigree dating back to late nineteenth-century artists – such as the English Lord Leighton (see Leighton House on page 85) and the American Hudson River painter Frederic Church – who filled their homes with a heady profusion of eastern and oriental objects including many examples of Persian and Turkish carpets.

The appeal is manifold, perhaps more so than ever before in this age of global telecommunications and a blurring of national identities. Although, of course, highly contrived, ethnic-style interiors offer a welcome escape and a chance to indulge one's imagination, whether one opts for a Wild West interior complete with Navajo rugs, or goes all out to recreate a scene from 'Arabian Nights' with an interior brimming with oriental textiles and carpets.

North Africa has long been a major source of inspiration and influence for artists; looking at the illustrations of Moroccan interiors (see page 121) and Tunisian interiors (see pages 114–115) it is easy to see why. For opulence and exoticism they are hard to beat. Creating an outdoor room (see pages 116 and 118–119) using carpets and cushions for entertaining is a delightfully imaginative idea and very easy to achieve. Even picnics could suddenly become fabulously exotic affairs with the addition of the odd easily transportable oriental rug.

Ethnic need not mean cluttered, as can be seen in the pared down simple rooms of the adobe houses of New Mexico (see pages 112–113). Weavings play an important part in such interiors, adding a splash of colour and texture, rather in the same way that tribal weavings do in eastern tribal societies. It is the essential purity of the designs that appeal – they are deeply rooted in the indigenous culture and are totally without outside influences. To a sophisticated cosmopolitan western eye, there is something inherently romantic and timeless about ethnic textile and carpet designs. Today they are venerated in the way in which early twentieth-century artists were inspired by African art. With a little bit of thought it is easy to integrate ethnic carpets into various different types of interior.

A twentieth-century Navajo rug woven for the tourist market sits harmoniously in this rugged Wild West-style American interior.

left: A 1920s Navajo rug in a rough-hewn frame dominates one wall beneath a gigantic Alaskan moose-antler chandelier in this log and stone 'cowboy castle' in Wyoming. Four bar stools in the same property *(right)* provide an impromptu seating area around the small kitchen.
above: Early twentieth-century Navajo rugs in the shop at the trading post, now a National Historic Site, established by Lorenzo Hubbell in the late nineteenth century in Arizona, just across the New Mexican border. The rear wall is hung with framed designs for Navajo blankets.

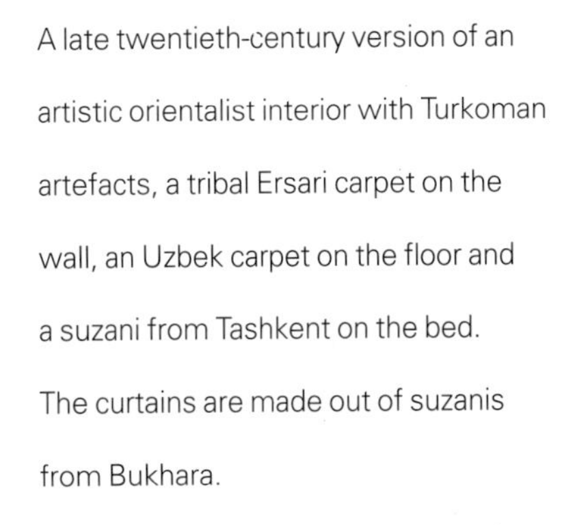

A late twentieth-century version of an artistic orientalist interior with Turkoman artefacts, a tribal Ersari carpet on the wall, an Uzbek carpet on the floor and a suzani from Tashkent on the bed. The curtains are made out of suzanis from Bukhara.

above: A carpet softens a billiard room in a South African house decorated by Hannes Myburg.
right: A pared-down bedroom in a house in Ibiza is softened by the use of flatwoven Moroccan carpets on the floor.
far right: A Caucasian striped rug, c.1880s, sits happily in a bedroom.

previous pages left: Cushions are piled on an Uzbek carpet, c.1900, with a fine Tekke Turkoman carpet, c.1920, as a backdrop in carpet and textile specialist Pip Rau's London home.

previous pages right: Covered sofas surround a 1930s Turkish kilim in a deliciously opulent exotic interior.

above left: Simple striped cotton rugs add a splash of colour and design in a kitchen in Michael Freeman's Rancho de las Golondrinas, near Taos, New Mexico.
above right: A colourful striped cotton rug is boldly arresting in an uncluttered interior typical of a New Mexican hacienda.

previous pages: An early twentieth-century North African carpet is used to enliven a tranquil interior in a Tunisian house. *above:* A typical modern Afghan carpet stylishly used to turn an outdoor terrace into a room in the Ibizan home of Rolf Blakstad, a Canadian architect and designer. The two carpets on the floor inside Blakstad's home *(right)* are Baluch brocaded flatweaves, c.1910, and a fine Ersari rug is hung on the back wall as decoration.

previous pages: A striking collection of tribal rugs including a Turkoman flatweave and several Turkish kilims, create an exotic atmosphere on a roof terrace in Marrakech, Morocco.

above: A Turkish brocaded carpet, c.1910, on the floor and an Afghan brocade, c.1920, over the seat add a note of comfort and pattern in a carefully contrived pared-down interior.

right: A modern Ladik rug adds greatly to a wonderfully exotic bedroom in Marrakech.

contemporary

There is a revolution taking place underfoot as more and more people are beginning to realise the huge decorative potential contemporary carpets can offer. Carpet designers have not had it so good since the 1920s and 1930s. At last their talents are being recognised and carpets in a modern idiom are again being awarded the accolades they so rightly deserve. It is an exciting time for anyone interested in expanding the boundaries of carpet design.

After the decorative excesses of the 1980s, the new millennium is being marked by the current vogue for relatively uncluttered interiors filled with a handful of carefully chosen decorative details. A contemporary rug is an obvious choice for such a pared-down look. Many of the rooms illustrated in this chapter are typical of this style and are a perfect background to the carpets depicted. It is a look that is particularly well suited to loft conversions. In its way this international cool chic style is just as much a refuge from the frenetic pace of late twentieth-century living as the rustic look.

Happily several carpet designers have been enlightened enough to bring out limited edition ranges of modern carpet and rug designs that are relatively inexpensive, which makes it an accessible look. Although this kind of carpet is likely to be gun-tufted as opposed to hand-knotted, the decorative appeal remains.

It is wrong to think that contemporary rugs can work only in ultra-modern settings, but it takes an experienced and sophisticated eye to have the confidence to use such rugs in settings where the more predictable choice might be to opt for a faded Persian carpet.

Another relatively unexplored way in which to use contemporary carpets is as wall hangings (see page 133). Rather like a stunning Mark Rothko would be hung on a wall as a dash of knock-out colour, why not treat carpets the same way? They have the bonus of adding warmth and texture to an interior.

It is a field that is developing all the time as more and more designers recognise the huge potential and the eager market for contemporary design that has emerged over the last few years.

'Arc Nero', a gun-tufted carpet by British carpet designer Helen Yardley, would make a bold decorating statement in any interior and would be equally effective whether used as a wall hanging or on the floor.

previous pages: Carpets designed by Jean Jacques Beaumé for Toulemonde-Bochart are used to great effect in a Parisian house boat.
left: A modern landscape painting, an antique native American Indian headdress and a striped flatweave sit happily side by side in this Wisconsin barn conversion.
above: A hooked 'fish' rug in the bathroom of a London house designed by Jean Oh Architects adds a splash of bold colour.

VANITY FAIR
HIMALAYAS

previous pages left: A handsome example of a carpet designed by Raymond Loewy, an American Art Deco designer, in a New York apartment.

previous pages right: A striking black and white chequerboard carpet in the Parisian drawing-room of a fashion designer.

left top: A carpet designed by Christopher Farr specifically for a London dining-room around a table and a set of dining chairs designed by Rupert Senior skilfully unites the overall decorative scheme.

left below and right (detail): A custom-made carpet in a London drawing room designed by June Hilton, a Denmark-based designer who finds inspiration in the culture of her childhood home in Alaska.

previous pages left: Ripples in a pool of water are the inspiration behind this rug by Judy Ross for Salon Moderne in a typically fashionable New York loft. In the same loft *(previous pages right)* great swirls of colour are an abstract representation of roses seen from above, in a hand-tufted woollen rug also by Judy Ross.

above: 'Blocks', a rug designed by Judy Ross for Salon Moderne and made in India, was inspired by the murals of the Ndebele women in South Africa. Here it is used to co-ordinate the overall colour scheme of a library in a New York loft conversion. *right:* A French interior decorated with elegant antiques standing on a twentieth-century carpet designed by Guy de Rougemont.

COCO
CHANEL

previous pages: A modern carpet made according to the measuring tape design which Eileen Gray created in collaboration with Jean Badovici for a house in Roquebrune, south France.

above: A heavily textured cream cotton dhurrie suits this 1960s style cave-like room in Italy.

right: Carpet designed by English textile designer Kate Blee for Christopher Farr in a London loft conversion by architects Proctor Matthews.

carpet types

a buyer's guide to oriental and western carpets

carpet types: an introduction

It would be impossible in a single volume to describe every kind of oriental and western carpet ever woven. The huge variety is both what makes the subject so exciting and at the same time intimidating to all but the specialist.

Given the huge range of carpet types to choose from, it is not surprising that the prospect of buying a carpet can be extremely daunting. This section begins with a few useful guidelines to bear in mind when setting out to purchase a carpet, followed by descriptions of the most widely seen carpet types, ranging from very rare antique oriental and western examples right up to the recent renaissance of interest of carpets which has led to exciting new collaborations between western designers and Near Eastern carpet producers. Although the early carpet types are often museum or rarefied collectors' pieces only, the most important types of these are included here, as they had a strong design influence on subsequent, more affordable types.

The main characteristics of the various carpets, including the design, the typical colours and motifs, the type of weave, as well as any specific individual features which help to identify a particular provenance, are discussed. In addition, practical issues are covered, such as whether the carpets come in specific sizes or formats, and whether or not they are hardwearing.

The terms 'carpet' and 'rug' are often confused – in the trade, a carpet must measure at least 1.8 x 2.7m (6' x 9'). Anything smaller should be classified as a rug. However in America, the term 'rug' is used as a blanket term to describe all but the very largest of pieces, which are referred to as 'carpets'.

Like so many things, carpets and rugs are subject to fashion and it can be difficult to gauge over a period of years what they are worth. However, antique carpets are becoming increasingly rare and consequently more and more expensive, and this can only continue with the passing of the years.The carpet market can be affected by several external factors, such as the political situation in the case of oriental carpets, typified by the embargo on Iranian goods, and hence Persian carpets, by the States since the Iranian revolution in 1979. Interior decorators are another important influence, as they

previous pages: Street scene in Morocco.

opposite: 'Carpet Bazaar, Cairo', 1887, by Charles Robertson (1844–91).

dictate what is fashionable and consequently boost the price of a particular carpet type. However, high quality, whether in terms of knot count, quality of weaving, or good design and colour use, overrides the dictates of fashion, and such carpets will always command top prices.

Buying a carpet

Buying a carpet tends to involve a considerable outlay, so it is wise not to rush any decision. Before setting out it is worth considering a few crucial points, such as the price you are prepared to pay; what kind of wear and tear the carpet will be subject to (a hall carpet is obviously going to suffer much heavier traffic than a bedside rug); what kind of colour palette is suitable, subtle or strong; whether you want a busy pattern or a configuration of large motifs and so on. Perhaps the most important decision is whether to buy a new carpet or an old (50–100 years) one, and if old, how worn and damaged a carpet you are

prepared to live with. The growing interest in and return to traditional methods of spinning, dying and weaving in the Near East mean that it is now possible to have relatively inexpensive copies of antique carpets made, which is well worth considering, as a modern reproduction of, say, an Indian Agra or French Aubusson can be made to a specific size and colourway, and still at a fraction of the price of an antique version. Another recent development has been the vogue for 'designer' carpets woven in Turkey to designs by leading fashion luminaries and contemporary artists such as Romeo Gigli or Georgina von Etzdorf for Christopher Farr, the British carpet designer and dealer.

In addition, although some contemporary carpets by modern designers are expensive because they are hand-dyed and hand-knotted by skilled workers, mostly in the Near East, some modern designers use a gun-tufting technique to make their carpets. Gun-tufting works on a principle akin to a stapler, shooting tufts of wool onto a canvas ground. A relatively quick and easy method to execute, it is inexpensive when compared with the cost of hand-woven carpets. The choice depends on your budget and preference.

Skeins of naturally dyed spun wool ready for weaving carpets under the DOBAG project in Turkey.

If buying an antique carpet, the condition is of paramount importance. To some people the concept of a carpet which shows its age by a low pile is anathema, whilst to others it is an attractive quality akin to the rich patina acquired on an antique piece of furniture. Obviously if buying as an investment it is wise to buy a carpet in good condition, unless it is an extremely rare example of a particular type, which you may choose to use as a wall hanging or table covering.

If you have decided to buy an antique carpet, it is a good idea to go to the auction houses, where it is possible to touch and closely examine the carpets for sale at leisure. The major auction houses all have carpet sales the same week twice a year. A caveat is that a modicum of knowledge or advice from a dealer or auction house expert is essential, as it is all too easy to make a mistake. There are a few things that you should be wary of if intending to purchase at auction, such as unwittingly buying a carpet that has been cut or assembled from different fragments.

The key to choosing a carpet is to train your eye. After a while you will find that you are instinctively attracted to certain types that you will start to recognise. As your eye is educated, be prepared to change your predilections. It is only natural that the more one knows about a certain subject the more discerning one becomes.

For those who do not have the opportunity to frequent the auction houses, there are reputable dealers on both sides of the Atlantic who are willing to devote considerable time showing and discussing their stock of carpets and rugs. Ask around – anyone who has been in the business for some time will have built up a certain reputation. Don't be intimidated by dealers. Remember it is in their interests to sell carpets at the right price as they have a reputation to keep and will want you to recommend them to all your friends. The International Directory at the back of the book provides useful information on recommended dealers.

Once you have picked out a few carpets which you like the look of, ask the dealer if you can take them home on approval. Don't be afraid to ask questions, as any good dealer will be happy to draw upon years of experience to advise you. All reputable dealers are insured and should be willing to let potential customers take the goods away for a few days on approval. In the same way that people pin up wallpaper samples, put down the carpets and see what they look like by day and by night. It is very hard in a dealer's shop to envisage what a particular carpet would look like in the context of one's home. It will quickly become apparent whether or not it works in the room. Above all, trust your instinct, and don't be swayed by what is deemed to be fashionable.

Beware anywhere that has a 'closing down' or 'bankrupt stock' notice. These may be cunning ploys to catch the naive buyer and many shops display such notices all year around. They are to be avoided at all costs, as are any warehouse auctions. They invariably sell hundreds of poor-quality carpets that are not worth considering.

Natural and chemical dyes

One should be wary of chemically dyed carpets which can be can be difficult to recognise: even experts have been known to be taken in as good chemical dyes mimic natural dyes perfectly. Another pitfall to watch out for is carpets which have been washed with a chemical dye. This process entails washing the carpet in a bleach or permanganate-based rinse to dull down or soften the colours, giving the rugs the superficial appearance of a false patina of age. Purchasing a carpet from a reputable dealer is the best way to steer clear of this problem.

All carpets and textiles that predate 1860 are naturally dyed. The natural dyes used to colour these weavings came from plants, minerals or animals. The colours were made fast to the wools or cottons by using a mordant, an additional dye used before or during the colouring process to prepare the wool. The intensity and depth of colour could be altered by the amount of mordant. Natural dyes create slightly irregular colour depth on wools so that when they are woven up into a carpet it is given a unique character achieved by the minute differences in hues within each colour. This characteristic is different from 'abrash' which is where the weaver working with one colour replaces it with another similar colour; the effect of this colour change is valued as an attractive quality in carpets. Natural dyes are lightfast, and mellow with time, whereas many chemical dyes are violent in colour and are prone to dramatic light fading in sunlight.

Chemical dyes were invented in the 1860s. The first chemical dyes were called aniline dyes which in turn were superseded by chrome dyes, which are widely used today. In many traditional oriental carpet-producing areas, the art of the master dyer was totally lost by the early twentieth century. Nowhere was this more pronounced than in Turkey, where chemical dyes were widespread by the late nineteenth and early twentieth centuries. For much of the twentieth century, the majority of oriental carpets, with the exception of certain nomadic weavings, are chemically dyed.

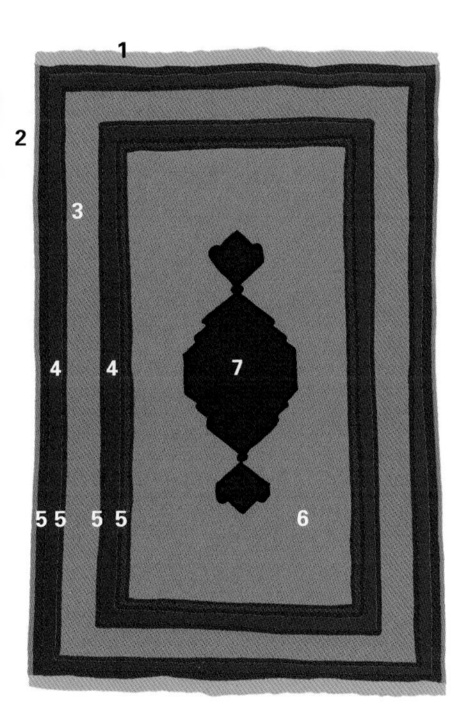

The main components of a carpet can be seen in this Feraghan rug, 1.3 x 1.95m (4'3" x 6'5"), c. 1856, from north-west Persia, which are numbered in the line drawing above:

1 fringe

2 selvedge

3 main border

4 minor borders

5 guard stripes

6 field

7 medallion

An introduction to oriental rugs

The majority of people setting out to buy an oriental carpet have only a vague idea as to what type of carpet they would like. The term 'oriental carpet' is a blanket one, embracing a vast range of styles which can be intimidating in its scope. In order to clarify the different types of oriental carpets most widely available and most suitable for furnishing the home, the following section is divided into countries and then into regions for the larger countries, which have their own distinctive weavings. Flatweaves, which includes kilims, one of the most popular choices of decorative oriental carpets, have their own section. There is a further section on contemporary carpets, which includes a selection of the best oriental carpets produced today with modern designs.

There are four very clearly demarcated carpet-making environments in the Orient, which partly explains the astonishingly diverse appearance of oriental carpets and the vast range of sizes. These are the tribal milieu, the village industry, the commercial workshops and the rarefied Islamic court ateliers. The latter were in operation during the sixteenth and seventeenth centuries, and surviving examples of carpets from the court ateliers are extremely rare. However, they are important to study because of the enormous influence they had on the design of later carpets in the other three groups.

In recent years tribal rugs and kilims have come to be recognised as an art form in their own right, worthy of being on a par with the best of ethnic art and craft. The huge growth in popularity of tribal rugs has meant that the criteria that a high knot count signifies the best quality has come to be questioned: if a knot is appropriate to a design then such carpets are now considered equal in quality to more finely woven pieces.

Tribal carpets appear not to have the sophisticated appeal of a court carpet, but their inherent feeling for pattern and colour can be just as beguiling. Woven from memory, the majority of tribal pieces were functional and used in everyday tribal life. Naturally the designs vary from area to area and many include symbols pertinent to a particular tribe.

Over the centuries, nomadic people in the Near East have settled in villages, bringing with them their tribal tradition of weaving, which soon became a source of income as opposed to something created for their own domestic use. Village weavers draw upon their tribal heritage, but are freer to experiment with patterns and colour palettes to appeal to buyers. A good example is the wonderfully inventive and strikingly coloured designs woven for sale by Caucasian village people in the second half of the nineteenth century. The majority of village production is done from memory, although very occasionally drawings or cartoons are used, but not with the scrupulous adherence to formula required by commercial workshops. The materials used are the same as those of the tribal weavers and the size of carpets is similar, rarely exceeding two-and-a-half metres (eight feet) in width. Village weavers sell their goods themselves whilst many become attached to a local merchant and weave specifically to order.

Commercial workshops are highly organised concerns, with all the different stages in the production of the carpet clearly allocated to different craftsmen, from the draughtsman responsible for the carpet designs or 'cartoons' to the weaver employed to execute them knot for knot. It is a process akin to a factory. Commercial workshop carpets tend to be larger pieces than either tribal or village production as they have the space for wider looms. The charming quirks so characteristic of tribal and village weaving are rarely in evidence in carpets from commercial workshops. By their nature, commercial workshop carpets are much slicker but can be very attractive – it is the design and colour that really marks out the best type. It was the late nineteenth century that witnessed the development of commercial workshops on a large scale, such as the Ziegler firm set up in Sultanabad in 1883.

The naming of rugs is often based on the market place where they were sold, to which weavers bring their pieces for sale from the surrounding area. Hence the name of origin is not always strictly accurate. Another point worth noting is that the terrain and climate can affect the nature of the carpets produced there. For instance, the climate of India is not conducive to sheep rearing, which explains the rarity of Indian woollen carpets, whereas it is suitable for growing cotton, hence the large-scale production of cotton dhurries. High altitudes produce thick pile carpets and lower altitudes a shorter pile.

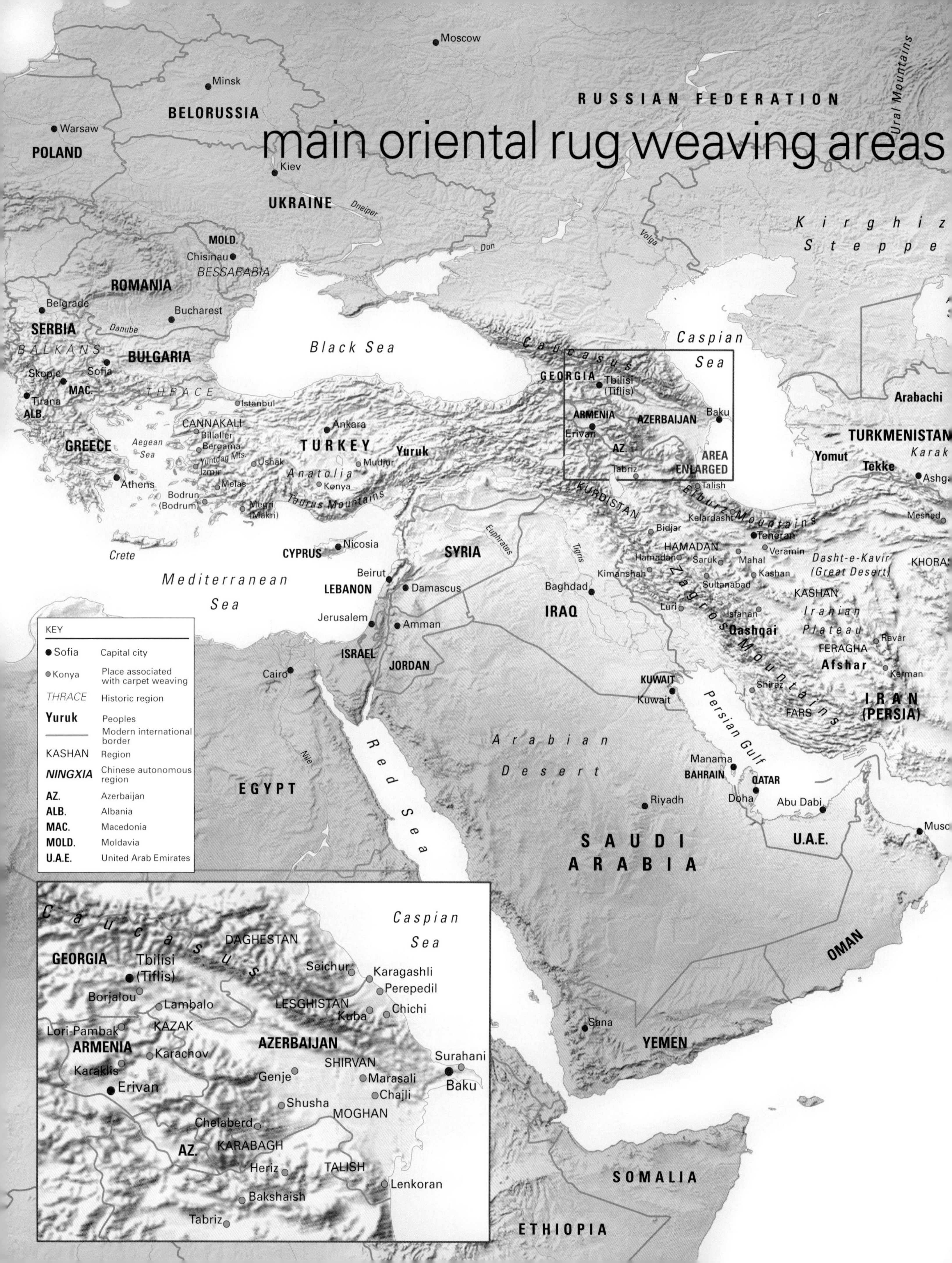
main oriental rug weaving areas
RUSSIAN FEDERATION
Moscow
Minsk
BELORUSSIA
Warsaw
POLAND
Kiev
UKRAINE
Dneiper
Ural Mountains
Kirghiz Steppe
Volga
Don
MOLD.
Chisinau
BESSARABIA
ROMANIA
Belgrade
Bucharest
SERBIA
Danube
BALKANS
BULGARIA
Sofia
Skopje
MAC.
Tirana
ALB.
THRACE
Black Sea
Caspian Sea
Caucasus
GEORGIA
Tbilisi (Tiflis)
ARMENIA
Erivan
AZERBAIJAN
Baku
AZ.
Tabriz
AREA ENLARGED
Arabachi
TURKMENISTAN
Yomut
Tekke
Karak
Ashga
Istanbul
CANNAKALE
Billaller
Bergama
Yuntdag Mts.
Izmir
Ushak
Melas
Bodrun (Bodrum)
Megri (Makri)
Ankara
TURKEY
Yuruk
Mudjur
Anatolia
Konya
Taurus Mountains
GREECE
Aegean Sea
Athens
Crete
CYPRUS
Nicosia
SYRIA
Euphrates
Tigris
KURDISTAN
Talish
Elburz Mountains
Kelardasht
Meshed
Bidjar
Teheran
HAMADAN
Hamadan
Saruk
Mahal
Veramin
Dasht-e-Kavir (Great Desert)
KHORAS
Kimanshah
Kashan
Sultanabad
KASHAN
Zagros Mountains
Baghdad
IRAQ
Luri
Isfahan
Iranian Plateau
Qashqai
Ravar
FERAGHA
Afshar
Kerman
Shiraz
FARS
IRAN (PERSIA)
Mediterranean Sea
Beirut
LEBANON
Damascus
Jerusalem
Amman
ISRAEL
JORDAN
Cairo
KUWAIT
Kuwait
Persian Gulf
Arabian Desert
Red Sea
Nile
EGYPT
Manama
BAHRAIN
QATAR
Doha
Abu Dabi
Riyadh
U.A.E.
Musc
SAUDI ARABIA
OMAN
Sana
YEMEN
SOMALIA
ETHIOPIA
KEY
Sofia Capital city
Konya Place associated with carpet weaving
THRACE Historic region
Yuruk Peoples
Modern international border
KASHAN Region
NINGXIA Chinese autonomous region
AZ. Azerbaijan
ALB. Albania
MAC. Macedonia
MOLD. Moldavia
U.A.E. United Arab Emirates
Caucasus
Caspian Sea
DAGHESTAN
GEORGIA
Tbilisi (Tiflis)
Seichur
Karagashli
Perepedil
Borjalou
Lambalo
LESGHISTAN
Kuba
Chichi
Lori-Pambak
KAZAK
ARMENIA
Karachov
AZERBAIJAN
Surahani
SHIRVAN
Karaklis
Genje
Marasali
Baku
Erivan
Chajli
Shusha
MOGHAN
Chelaberd
AZ.
KARABAGH
Heriz
TALISH
Lenkoran
Bakshaish
Tabriz

RUSSIAN FEDERATION
Irtysh
Ishim
Astana
ZAKHSTAN
Altai Mountains
Ulan Bator
MONGOLIA
Lake Balkhash
Syr Darya
URKESTAN
Urumqi
Tien Shan
Turfan
Bishkek
Kucha
KYRGYZSTAN
Tashkent
Aksu
Lop Nur
XINJIANG UYGHUR ZIZHIQU
Samarkand
Kashgar
TAJIKISTAN
Dushanbe
Pamirs
Takla Makan Desert
Amu Darya
Yarkand
Khotan
Keriya
Niya
Kunlun Shan
Qinghai Hu
Lanzhou
Hindu Kush
KASHMIR
CHINA
NINGXIA
Kabul
Srinagar
Islamabad
ANISTAN
TIBET
[XIZANG ZIZHIQU]
PUNJAB
Lahore
Amritsar
Plateau of Tibet
Himalayas
Lhasa
PAKISTAN
New Delhi
NEPAL
Kathmandu
Thimpu
BHUTAN
Jaipur
Agra
Thar Desert
RAJASTHAN
Brahmaputra
Ganges
Mirzapur
Indus
BANGLADESH
INDIA
Dhaka
BURMA
LAOS
abian
Sea
Western Ghats
Deccan
Bay of Bengal
Eastern Ghats
Rangoon
THAILAND
DIAN
EAN
Bangkok
INDIAN OCEAN
Andaman Is.
Nicobar Is.
SRI LANKA

persia

Of all the centres of carpet production in the Orient, none equals Persia (modern-day Iran) for its rich diversity of designs, colour and weave. A Persian carpet has long been considered as the apogee of everything an exotic oriental carpet should be.

As early as the fourteenth century, fine carpets were an integral part of sophisticated Persian court life. Beautifully detailed miniatures show brightly coloured geometric patterned carpets as often the sole item of furnishing. The carpets were used to decorate the floors of palaces, mosques and sometimes even garden pavilions. An Italian visitor to the summer palace of Shah Abbas (1587–1629) describes an opulent open-air evening reception with chandeliers, soft music and rich carpets spread out for guests.

Ever since Persian carpets first made their appearance in seventeenth-century Europe via the ancient silk route and through ports on Persia's southern coasts, they have been venerated as objects of great beauty and fine workmanship. Leading artists of the day such as Rubens, Vermeer, de Hooch and Van Dyck depicted Persian carpets in their pictures. The carpets are mostly shown covering tables as it was not until the seventeenth century that carpets began to be widely used as floor coverings.

The 'golden age' of the Persian carpet spanned the sixteenth and seventeenth centuries. Persia was conquered by the Safavids in 1499 and it was Shah Tahmasp, crowned in 1514, who was instrumental in setting up royal workshops specialising in the production of textiles and carpets, notably at Kashan, Kerman, Isfahan and Tabriz. Hitherto the weavers in the existing carpet workshops had probably been responsible for all aspects of carpet design, but in the new court ateliers they often worked with court miniaturists and book illuminators. The miniaturists brought their inherently highly disciplined approach to bear on the composition of the designs, imbuing them with a strong sense of rhythmically controlled patterns whilst retaining a painterly eye. The ensuing designs are astonishingly sophisticated and beautiful to behold. An appealing aspect of many of the carpets produced during this period was the designers' desire to portray the symbolic Muslim vision of Paradise as a lush garden on their carpets. Many carpets are visions of a magically fertile world teeming with birds and animals set amongst graceful arabesques, flowers, trees and calligraphy. Considered against the arid environment in which they were produced, they appear even more luxurious and fabulous. The skilled weaving required to render the finely graduated curves of an arabesque using the asymmetrical or Persian knot, a finer knot than the symmetrical or Turkish knot, are a good indication of the consummate art of rug weavers working under the Safavid Dynasty.

The few Persian carpets that survive from this period are highly prized and can be seen in stately homes, museums and royal palaces in Europe and America. Over the centuries they have been a major source of influence for many subsequent carpet designers, notably William Morris who was inspired by the world famous sixteenth-century Ardebil carpet which he was instrumental in advising the Victoria and Albert Museum to buy in 1893, as well as the Chelsea carpet in his capacity as an Art Referee. The Ardebil carpet cost £2,000, a fantastic price for the time and a clear indication of the esteem with which it was held even then.

But Persian carpets are not just confined to the rarefied world of court ateliers. There is an equally long tradition of carpets being woven by urban workshops, remote villages and nomadic camps. As is to be expected, these carpets are much more direct and simple in coloration and pattern and often smaller than the elegant formality of the court carpets, appealing to a totally different eye.

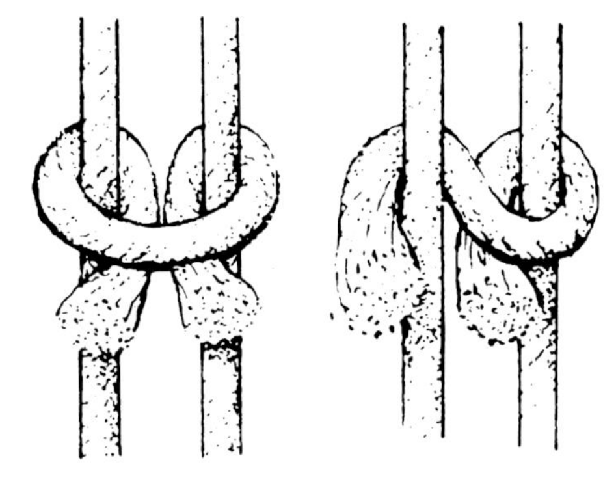

above, left: Symmetrical or Turkish knot; *above, right:* Asymmetrical or Persian knot. *left:* Qashqai (detail), 1.75 x 2.4m (5'9" x 8'), nineteenth century.

Most illustrations in this section are © David Black. Special thanks also to John Eskenazi, C. John, Kennedy Carpets, Clive Loveless and Alberto Levi.

After the demise of the Safavids and the invasion of the Afghans in 1722, the quality of Persian carpet production declined, and it is not until what is sometimes referred to as the revival period, during the second half of the nineteenth century, that Persian carpets are again worth studying.

In the nineteenth century, there was a burgeoning mercantile class in Europe looking for new goods with which to furnish their homes. The greatly improved communications with the Orient, coupled with the popular quest for oriental exoticism, led to the setting up of carpet production centres in Persia specifically geared to manufacturing carpets in their hundreds for the western market. The first such firm was the English company Ziegler, which was founded by an astute Manchester entrepreneur, Philip Ziegler. He set up an agency in 1883 in Sultanabad (Arak), a town situated in west central Persia, in the centre of the weaving area that produced Mahal and Feraghan carpets. A thriving export market was rapidly established, and carpets were soon being shipped back by the boatload to England, where they were rapidly snapped up and became generically known as 'Zieglers'. Other European and American companies quickly followed suit and many maintained offices in Sultanabad until the 1920s. Hitherto a major problem with carpets imported from the East had been that their sizes were not suitable for western interiors. Many of the carpets were a type known as 'Kelleh', and were long and thin. The new Ziegler type carpets were specifically woven in sizes acceptable to the West, usually in large rectangles.

Innovative fashionable shops of the day, such as Liberty of London which was established in 1875, and whose carpet department was opened in 1885, were instrumental in disseminating the vogue for Persian carpets specially woven for the western market. There was a network of people working for Liberty all over the Orient.

At the same time a number of dealers quickly established a thriving market for Persian carpets in the West. The late nineteenth century was a great period of widespread country house building by a band of successful entrepreneurs throughout Europe, all of which needed to be decorated with carpets.

The carpet department at Liberty, Gresham House, 142–144 Regent Street, London, was opened in 1885 and retailed carpets and furniture.

The outbreak of the First World War curtailed the trading activities of the majority of carpet merchants, although some firms managed to keep offices going in far-flung parts of the Orient until well into the 1920s. Over the next few decades, standards declined dramatically, crude chemical dyes (known as aniline dyes), first introduced in the 1860s, were increasingly widely used and the industry became more and more commercialised to the extent that weavers were given patterns that were often not

Lavar Kerman (detail), 6.1 x 8.5m (20′ x 27′10″), late nineteenth century.

from their area and the quality of design then deteriorated. This happened from the second half of the nineteenth century onwards. The early aniline dyes were increasingly used from around 1875 and the early years of the twentieth century, and carpets dating from this period often have a mixture of natural and chemical colours. Whereas the natural colours have kept their vibrancy, the chemical ones have often faded to a dirty grey. The ensuing results have none of the vitality of carpets produced by weavers working to methods and designs passed down through the generations.

In many areas of Persia the degenerative qualities of these dyes were noted by the authorities and measures were taken to omit them from carpet production, including punitive taxes on their import. Aniline dyes were gradually superseded by the more light-fast chrome dyes which are still widely used today.

Since the mid-1980s there has been a renaissance of interest in traditional methods in Iran. This is because the subtle colours of vegetable dyes, as opposed to the garish colours of poor chemical dyes, are beginning to be appreciated, and there is a general swing towards individual handcraftsmanship after decades of rejection. Vegetable dyes are once again beginning to be used and many weavers are returning to historic patterns. A few individuals including the late Shah of Iran's wife, who set up a weaving school at Shiraz using vegetable dyes, have been enlightened enough to realise that something must be done to ensure the survival of what was once a great tradition producing magnificent carpets. Another example is in Teheran where the Miri Iranian Rugs company, in the carpet business since the 1820s, began to experiment in 1987 with the weavers of Kelardasht in northern Iran, where the local carpet industry was nearly extinct. The Miri company had to supply the weavers with patterns traditional to the area. Now more than 3,000 people in over a dozen towns in the provinces of Fars, Kashan, Kurdistan and Hamadan are involved in the scheme.

Tabriz (detail), 3.4 x 4.2m (11'2" x 13'9"), c. 1880.

Floral designs

Tabriz

There is a long tradition of carpet weaving in Tabriz, a town in north-west Persia in the Turkish-speaking province of Azerbaijan. It is best known as a major centre of finely woven carpets during the nineteenth-century revival period.

The knotted-pile carpets produced by a network of town workshops are generally wool, finely woven and are fairly stiff to handle. Not so common are silk rugs including some with metallic thread. A central medallion surrounded by arabesques and floral motifs and corner patterns are frequently found in Tabriz carpets (see example). Hunting scenes are not uncommon. Often the original colours have faded to a browny/coral pink with an ivory ground colour. Tabriz are popular with interior decorators, particularly those in pale colours. Modern Tabriz carpets use modern production methods such as chemical dyes and machine-spun wool.

Kerman

Situated in south-east Persia, Kerman (Kirman) was one of the towns where the Safavids set up a court atelier. It has remained an important centre of carpet production ever since, particularly over the last century. An interesting influence during the nineteenth century was the town's tradition of woollen shawl production. Many local weavers produced beautifully woven shawls decorated with designs based on the floral-cone motif, the boteh, known in Europe as Paisley. As the demand for shawls declined, partly explained by the fact that by the late nineteenth century, similar shawls were being produced in Paisley, Scotland, the weavers were smart enough to adapt their skills to the increasingly popular skill of carpet weaving with successful results. Not surprisingly the floral-cone motif is frequently to be seen in Kerman carpets in numerous

above, top: Kashan, 1.2 x 2.2m (4' x 7'3"), late nineteenth century.
below: Meshed, 3.9 x 5.7m (12'9" x 18'9"), early twentieth century.

permutations. It is often hard to pinpoint exactly what constitutes a Kerman design , as the motifs and patterns used are typical of many centres of Persian carpet production. Floral medallions and corner motifs are popular, as are flowering tree patterns and pictorial hunting designs. Pale washed-out colours such as beige and white are typical.

The Lavar example illustrated on page 155 is a very finely knotted large piece, with an unusual overall small floral pattern on an ivory field. It was possibly made specially to order. Lavar is now the accepted term for carpets produced in Ravar, near Kerman. Lavar was originally a misspelling. They are a particular kind of Kerman which, although quite rare, are famous for the superb quality of the weave. Typically woven in pinky colours, Lavars are very popular in America.

Kashan

In the Middle Ages, the town of Kashan in west central Persia was the centre of the Persian silk textile industry. A few exquisite silk carpets dating from the first half of the sixteenth century survive and are consummate examples of the sophisticated and beautifully drawn designs which were produced by the court miniaturists for carpets.

By the eighteenth century, there was little if any weaving in Kashan. It was not until the revival period that fine carpets once again began to be produced in Kashan, some woollen, some silk, and a number woven with a mixture of wool and silk. Typical designs have a central diamond-shaped medallion set in a densely patterned ground featuring arabesques often with spandrels to the corners (see glossary). A few silk carpets are still produced today including a style known as 'raised silk Kashan', in which the design is woven in pile on a flatweave ground, sometimes embossed with metal. These are show pieces and not very practical. There are two typical colour palettes of Kashan, one using a strong combination of dark reds and blues (madder and indigo); the other in more subdued pastel hues which are often referred to as 'blonde' or 'white' Kashans.

Meshed

The principal town in the region of Khorasan in north-west Persia is another place which underwent a renaissance of carpet weaving in the late nineteenth-century revival period, after a long period of the craft being in abeyance following the Afghan invasion of 1722. To this day it is still a major centre of carpet production. The carpets tend to

be densely patterned with graceful arabesques and either circular or oval medallions with corresponding spandrels in a rich palette of madder reds and blues.

Veramin

Situated just south-east of Teheran, Veramin has long been a melting-pot of many tribal groups including the Turkoman, Qashqai, Shahsevan, Lurs and Kurds, as well as an indigenous settled Persian population. Like Teheran, Veramin's carpet-weaving tradition did not really get going until the late nineteenth century. The carpets are tightly woven in superb rich colours with quite formal designs, often with large flower-heads and with a beautiful light turquoise colour dominating the field patterns (see example, left). Early Veramin carpets are much sought after as their designs are freer than recent productions. Veramin weavings come in the form of rugs, runners and also kilims.

above, top: Veramin, 1.5 x 2.7m (5' x 9'), late nineteenth century.
below: Bidjar, 1.2 x 2.1m (4' x 7'), nineteenth century.

Saruk

Finely woven small rugs are to be found in Saruk, a town in north-west Persia about 40 kilometres (25 miles) north of Arak. The weaving is much admired for its fineness and subtlety of design, which is similar in execution to the equally admired Feraghans. Few Saruk carpets of any size can be found today. The colours of Saruk carpets tend to be gentle like the coral-ground example illustrated opposite. The red dyes can be fugitive, and blue wefts are common.

Bakshaish

The carpets produced at the beginning of the twentieth century in the small village of Bakshaish near Heriz in north-west Persia were produced in quiet colours which suit modern decorating tastes. They are usually finely woven, with bold open designs. The example shown is a small piece with an attractive yellow ground, and is exceptionally delicate with an inscription in the border, suggesting that it was for an important person.

Bidjar

Carpets made in the area around Bidjar in north-west Persia are the most robust of any oriental carpets, because of the weavers' characteristic technique of beating the

above: Saruk, 3.6 x 6m (12′ x 20′), late nineteenth century.
right: Bakshaish, 1 x 1.8m (3′6″ x 6′), c. 1890.

above, top: Afshar flame design rug, 1 x 1.5m (3'6" x 5'), nineteenth century. *below:* Mahal, 3.35 x 4.6m (11' x 15'), 1890s.

weft into place with a long iron bar, which is inserted between the warps during weaving then pounded against the wefts. The designs are usually typical nineteenth-century Persian in style and produced in a rectilinear format. Red or cream grounds combined with a strong light or dark blue are typical. Synthetic dyes were not introduced in Bidjar carpets until after the First World War. Because of their great strength (when wet a Bidjar is impossible to fold), they are suitable for areas of heavy wear in the home, such as hallways or landings. Bidjar carpets were made in a range of sizes, and can be very large.

Afshar

The Afshar are a Turkish-speaking people originally from Azerbaijan, of whom some are now settled and a few are semi-nomadic. Although they were ejected from their homelands as long ago as the sixteenth century, to this day their designs still clearly show a strong Azerbaijan, as well as a discernible Caucasian, influence. The multiple border designs are repeated in many Afshar rugs. The weavers do not weave from a pattern in front of them, but instead rely on their visual memory, incorporating stylised flowers and animals motifs and symbols in a great variety of colours passed down through the centuries. The example illustrated is a flame design, whose delightful use of golden yellow, red and black makes it instantly recognisable as an Afshar. Afshar carpets are slightly more subdued than those of the Qashqai, who are their neighbours in western Persia. Afshar rugs are square in shape with a deeply ribbed back.

Mahal

The large open designs using traditional motifs that feature in many Mahal carpets are reminiscent of Ziegler carpets, but they are more affordable. Natural dyes continued to be used on Mahal carpets for a longer period than on other Persian rugs. Workshops run by European firms made many of the older Mahals. The example shown is typical of the better type of Mahal, with a charming open design and palmettes in the Ziegler style.

above, left: Kirmanshah, 3 x 5.2m (9'9" x 17'), c. 1880.
right: Modern Persian rug in a traditional Persian design, by the Teheran company Miri Iranian Rugs.

Kirmanshah

The town of Kirmanshah is in north-west Persia, and should not be confused with the similar-sounding weaving town of Kerman, which is in the south-east. Kirmanshah rugs were at their best during the nineteenth-century revival period, and were not produced in great numbers, which is reflected in their high price. The example shown is fairly typical in its cypress tree motifs and the pinky-red background colour. Another typical Kirmanshah style is the 'garden' or 'compartment' design.

Modern Persian rugs

The Miri Iranian Rugs company was the first major producer of new carpets in Iran to use vegetable dyes, in rugs woven to high standards and incorporating traditional designs, some adapted from traditional motifs but still pleasing to the eye. This family firm based in Teheran has been producing carpets based on nineteenth-century examples since 1987. Miri represent the beginning of an important revival, producing carpets of a quality that have not appeared for more than a hundred years.

Geometric designs

Heriz

Heriz is a generic term which is used to describe carpets made in the town of Heriz in north-west Persia and the surrounding villages.

One of the best and most easily recognisable of all Persian carpet types, Heriz carpets have a very direct appeal, being extremely decorative in design. Many are coarsely woven and are consequently very robust. Bold exuberant geometric designs with a dominant central medallion or overall designs with a field of geometrically stylised floral forms are typical. Bright colours: brick reds, burnt orange and tangerine – all shades that come from madder dyes – and blues predominate, set off by contrasting shades of beige, ivory and yellow ochre. The bold wide borders are a defining characteristic, consisting of flowerheads that are found in many variations: angular, geometric and naturalistic.

Relatively near Tabriz, Heriz was also caught up in the late nineteenth-century revival period. The vigour and strong colours of Heriz proved extremely popular with the western taste of that period and blended in perfectly with their decorating schemes. They are just as popular today and are relatively easy to acquire. Interestingly they are more in demand in the West than in Persia, as Persians tend to go for a slightly finer woven carpet.

above, top: Heriz (detail), 4 x 4.6m (13′ x 15′), late nineteenth century.

below: Ziegler, 4 x 4.6m (13′ x 15′), c. 1880.

Ziegler

Highly sought after, Ziegler or Sultanabad carpets are hard to find and as a result very expensive. They typically feature great open designs uncharacteristic of other Persian nineteenth-century carpets. The best known is a pattern composed of large detached

Feraghan, 1.4 x 2.1m (4'6" x 7'), nineteenth century.

floral motifs scattered throughout the field. The innovation of expanding small detailed designs into a much larger format produced the famous Ziegler look which is always bold with the use of strong motifs, particularly palmettes (see glossary), beautifully spaced on a plain field. Yellow, blue, green and madder and coral red are the most typical colours. The piece shown uses typical Ziegler colours, and the very large palmettes and openly spaced design of the border is characteristic. Less typical is the highly detailed field.

Feraghan

Feraghan carpets were highly fashionable in the nineteenth century, particularly in England, where many are still to be seen in historic houses, museums and private collections. Feraghans are regarded as among the finest Persian rugs to be woven in the nineteenth century. They are finely woven with good quality wool and sophisticated designs, they are also very durable, which helps to explain their popularity.

Feraghans have distinctive 'showing-off' characteristics. The typically wide borders are often magnificent, with small guard stripes and a pistachio green ground colour. The copper vitriol used to make the green colour has a corrosive effect which can be felt if one runs one's hand over the carpet, where the pile has been corroded down.This explains the often etched appearance of many Feraghans. Reds and a golden yellow are also typical. The centre is usually com-

above: Qashqai, 1.2 x 2m (4' x 6'6"), nineteenth century. *right:* Hamadan, 0.9 x 1.5m (3' x 5'), c. 1860.

Qashqai, 1.67 x 2.4m (5'6" x 8'), nineteenth century.

posed of an all-over tightly controlled Herati pattern composed of what seems to be a floral design, but on closer inspection usually reveals itself to be a geometrical motif. The white ground of the example illustrated on page 163 denotes the importance of the piece, which was probably produced and woven for a khan, perhaps by Mustafa Hafiz, the famous nineteenth-century Persian rug designer.

Hamadan

Hamadan carpets are instantly recognisable due to the high proportion of plain camel hair used in the outer border, as seen in the example opposite, where the beautiful 'abrash', or tone variation, in the camel colour is very effective. The designs are similar to those of Caucasian rugs made to the north of Iran, with medallion and anchor designs in many different permutations being typical. Many Hamadan carpets come in the form of runners, and few large carpets were made. Hamadans have long been popular in the American market.

Qashqai

The Qashqai from the Fars district in south-west Persia (see map on pages 150–151) annually migrate to the Zagros mountains with their flocks of sheep and goats. They weave very fine semi-geometric designs, often filling the field of their carpets with animals and flowers. The sophistication of their weavings is particularly impressive if one remembers that all their work is produced by tent dwellers living in harsh desert conditions.

Baluch with 'tarantula' hooked design, 2.4 x 4m (8' x 13'), c1860.

The three Qashqai rugs illustrated demonstrate the rich variety of types produced by the tribe. The piece on page 165 depicts a whole world of animals – lions, tigers, dogs, birds – as well as thousands of flowers, and demonstrates the great skill of the weaver who would have worked entirely from memory and improvised as he wove. The example on page 152 illustrates the 'boteh' or seed design, in colours of deep madder red, rich golden yellow and ultramarine, all colours loved by the Qashqai weavers. The piece illustrated on page 164 shows the boteh design again, this time forming a 'mille-fleurs' pattern of great sophistication.

Baluch

Confusingly, the Baluchi tribes do not originate from the area called Baluchistan, which lies to the south-west of what is now Pakistan. The finest Baluchi rugs come from the large Afghan–Persian border district several hundred kilometres north of Baluchistan.

The majority of Baluch production was small rugs easily transportable by this nomadic people. Prayer rugs with a mihrab field and a tree-of-life pattern are one of the best-known of Baluch designs. The typical combination of dark colours, predominantly deep tones of red and blue, but also black (produced by using natural wool darkened with indigo dye) and brown, with small amounts of white looked particularly effective in the dark Baluchi tent interiors.

Large Baluchi carpets such as the example illustrated are quite rare, because as nomadic tent dwellers, the looms had to be small and easily transportable. The size of this carpet and its richness of design and fine execution suggests that it was probably made for a khan.

Gabbehs

Persian gabbehs are made by nomadic people in southern Persia. Although crude, they appeal to collectors of tribal weaving because of their simplicity and naive charm. The designs of contemporary gabbehs date back to the nineteenth century, demonstrating the respect shown by oriental weavers for past traditions.

The example from Luri in south-west Persia illustrated is a fine nineteenth-century piece, displaying a strong graphic quality of design with its three large diamond motifs, zigzag borders and simple colour use.

Luri gabbeh,

south-west Persia,

1.3 x 2m (4'3" x 6'5"),

late nineteenth century.

turkey

Melas prayer rug (detail), 1.5 x 2.1m (5' x 7'), nineteenth century.

The mention of a Turkey carpet automatically summons up an image of the predominantly scarlet, green and blue richly patterned carpets that were mass-produced for the West at the end of the nineteenth century. But this is to do Turkey a great injustice, as it has a long tradition of weaving since the days of the Seljuks' arrival from Central Asia in the thirteenth and fourteenth centuries. It was from Turkey that the first carpets arrived in the West in the sixteenth century. Carpets of Turkish origin appeared so frequently in paintings by the leading artists of the day that certain types of carpet styles became known as 'Lotto', 'Holbein' or 'Memling', labels which have stuck to this day.

Sophisticated carpets were produced for the Ottoman court in the sixteenth century in urban court workshop environments. Although there was a tradition of large carpets in Turkey from the thirteenth century onwards, equally important is the production from thousands of villages all over this huge country. Turkey has been traversed by numerous different nomadic tribes over the centuries, many of whom have settled relatively recently in village communities. They weave their own distinctive, boldly coloured, usually geometric patterns peculiar to their region or tribe. Confusingly in the carpet trade, Turkish carpets are often referred to as Anatolian. Anatolia is more or less the area covered by modern Turkey and is a geographical term for the land mass of Asia Minor. The age-old tradition of donating carpets to mosques to celebrate family events meant that it used to be possible to follow the history of Turkish carpet weaving. Sadly, the increased demand for rare early carpets has led to many mysterious disappearances of carpets from mosques, with the result that only a handful of carpets remain in the mosques to which they were given. Today nearly all the old carpets in mosques are being replaced by modern machine-made and chemically dyed carpets.

Many villages were established by settled nomads in the nineteenth century. To this day, the village designs being woven can in many cases be traced back to the fifteenth century. Obviously, contemporary examples are not identical, but there are clear threads connecting the carpets through the centuries.

As anyone who has examined the carpets for sale in the Grand Bazaar in Istanbul will have discovered, there is still a great number of chemically dyed crudely woven carpets

Bergama (detail), 1.67 x 1.95m (5'6" x 6'5"), nineteenth century

being touted. Every merchant will boast that his rugs are dyed with natural vegetable dyes, but this will frequently prove not to be the case. Take care. The poor quality of the lighting in the Grand Bazaar makes a torch an essential prerequisite if one is to examine the carpets carefully. One or two enlightened shopkeepers in the Grand Bazaar do stock carpets which are produced with natural vegetable-dyed wool, but this is the exception rather than the rule.

The recent revival of carpet weaving in Turkey specifically for the western market was led by the DOBAG project, begun in 1981, which commissions dyers and weavers skilled in traditional methods to produce top-quality traditional Turkish carpets. The two DOBAG carpets illustrated in this chapter show just how successful the results can be.

Geometric designs

Bergama

Known as Pergamon in ancient and modern times, Bergama on the Aegean coast is believed to have been the location where Holbein carpets were made in the fifteenth and sixteenth centuries. Today the few surviving examples can be seen in museum collections. More accessible are the village-woven pile rugs which are rarely larger than 1.5 x 2.1m (5' x 7'). Deep madder red dyes dominate the typical palette, but several other colours are used in smaller quantities, and some nineteenth-century examples are found with deep kilim flatweave skirts in plain red with yellow and black finishing stripes at either end (see illustration). They are quite coarsely woven with fairly thick pile and are rather floppy. The example shown uses a discreet apricot red in the main field, and the two interlocking medallions are distinctive Bergama design features.

Melas

Just north of Bodrun on the south-west Turkish coast, Melas is best known for its unusual prayer rugs, with their distinctive waisted prayer arch in a head-and-shoulders

above, top: Konya, 1.7 x 2.6m (5′ x 7′), early nineteenth century.

below: Mudjur prayer rug, 1.3 x 1.8m (4′5″ x 6′), mid-nineteenth century.

shape (see piece on page 168). Madder red is the main colour, along with a brightly hued yellow, as well as oranges, tans and small amounts of dark tones, usually with a shade of deep purple.The characteristic size of Melas rugs is around 2.1 x 1.5m (7′ x 5′).

Konya

Konya has the oldest tradition of carpet weaving in Anatolia. Konya rugs typically display powerful simple designs, often in a trellis design as in the example shown, where each compartment is filled with step-hooked polygons. The use of a warm yellow is a very strong feature. They are quite coarsely woven, but the weave suits the style of design. The rugs have a strong visual impact, rather in the way that Caucasian rugs do. The rug illustrated is in exceptional condition and the wide kilim ends are found on all late eighteenth- and early nineteenth-century pieces, denoting high weaving standards.

Mudjur

The settled nomads of Mudjur in central Turkey are best known for their prayer rugs which were woven in prodigious numbers. They are easily recognised by their wide main border which is made of repeating squares containing a floral diamond medallion. The deep madder red mihrab (as seen in the example illustrated) is very common, as are strong yellows and warm lime greens.

Megri

Located in the southernmost tip of western Anatolia, Megri (Makri) carpets are easily recognised by their double-column designs, curiously sometimes known as 'Rhodes'. The most frequently found are split into two halves, making double columns with different designs in each panel, one of them almost always containing a toothed lozenge repeating down a central spine (on the left-hand column in the example shown). Yellow predominates, as do strong blues and greens.

Yuruk

The Yuruk are unique in that they are the only settled nomads in eastern Anatolia. The rugs are woven with a very good quality wool using a long shaggy pile. The vividly hued colours include violet, yellow ochre, umber, sienna and the more traditional red, blue

above: Megri, 1.4 x 2.3m (4'6" x 7'6"), mid-nineteenth century.

right: Yuruk, 1 x 1.7m (3'5" x 5'7"), mid-nineteenth century.

above: DOBAG carpet, 1.75 x 2.6m (5'9" x 8'6"), 1994.

right: DOBAG carpet (detail), 3.6 x 5.4m (12' x 17'8"), 1994.

and green. The designs are based on different renditions of hexagons, medallions, diamonds, and hooked or stepped lozenges, as well as zigzag patterning in both the border and the field. The example shown uses natural camel wool, which is unusual. Its floating medallions are particularly striking.

DOBAG

The DOBAG project (an acronym deriving from the Turkish words for research and development into natural dyes) is largely the vision of Dr Harrald Böhmer of Marmara University in Istanbul, in conjunction with the university's textile department. They have been responsible for reintroducing the traditional dyeing and weaving techniques to villages on the Aegean coast in western Turkey since 1981. Two centres of production

above, top: Ushak, 4.3 x 5.5m (14' x 18'), c. 1900.

below: Ushak, 3.65 x 4.9m (12' x 16'), late nineteenth century.

have been set up there, one around the Cannakali region and the other in the Yuntdag mountains near Izmir.

All the carpets made under this project are based on antique designs. The colours are produced from natural dyes, and can seem surprisingly bright to eyes used to faded antique naturally dyed carpets or chemically bleached, synthetically dyed carpets, but they are testimony to the great skill of the dyers, as it is difficult to produce colours that are both natural and vibrant. The carpets quickly acquire a lovely patina and so improve with use and age.

The superb DOBAG rugs illustrated will still be cherished and enjoyed in a hundred years' time, and with correct care will remain in excellent condition, because the lanolin produced naturally from the hand-spun wool has not been removed, as occurs when wool is machine spun, as it is with many inferior modern rugs. The lanolin prevents the wool from becoming brittle and thus damaged.

The four parts of a compass design of the yellow and red rug is traditionally Turkish, and the rug was made in the Cannakali area of Turkey. The blue star motif DOBAG rug is from the village of Billaller, again in the Cannakali region, and the star motif is a traditional one from that area. Although the rug is relatively coarsely woven, the design reads with great clarity.

Floral designs

Ushak

Ushak, which is in west central Turkey, is an ancient commercial carpet-weaving centre, most famous for its 'star' and 'medallion' patterned rugs of the seventeenth and eighteenth centuries. These were venerated in Europe at the time, and often appear in contemporary paintings.

Ushak today produces little of merit, but carpets from the nineteenth and early twentieth centuries tend to be of very good quality and are highly sought after.

The red-ground Ushak displays excellent detailing, both in its endless field design and in the green border, and is a highly sophisticated piece.

The carpet with the white ground illustrated contains a design of heavily stylised linked geometric leaves, one of the designs frequently found in Ushak carpets.

the caucasus

above, top: Kazak 'sunburst' or 'eagle' design, 1.45 x 2.35m (4'9" x 7'8"), mid-nineteenth century.
below: Kazak 'cloudband' design, 1.58 x 2m (5'2" x 6'9"), nineteenth century.

The Caucasus region, some 160,000 square miles in area, is sandwiched between Turkey, Iran and Russia and stretches from the Black Sea in the west to the Caspian Sea in the east. The silk route ran along the shores of the Caspian Sea.

The turbulent history of the Caucasus, stretching back for more than eight hundred years until the Russian conquests of the late eighteenth and nineteenth centuries, is a long-running saga of ethnic, cultural and religious strife. A multitude of races including Turks, Arabs, Tartars, Mongols, Persians and Russians were constantly conquering or re-conquering the land. Stability never lasted for any length of time. For the carpet enthusiast it presents a challenging but exciting area to study, and furthermore one that was surprisingly neglected until relatively recently.

The ethnic richness and vast variety of designs to be found among Caucasian rugs and carpets can be ascribed to its history and the fact that hundreds of tribes are to be found in the Caucasus, speaking multifarious dialects. An indication of the complexity of the area is well illustrated by S. Zerimov in his study 'Azerbaijan Carpets', in which he lists 123 villages in the southern and mid-Caucasus alone that produced carpets of distinctive design. All Caucasian rugs are small and colourful and therefore easy to integrate in any room. They are immediately accessible to the novice studying oriental carpets. Designs are bold, uncomplicated and memorable, differing from their Persian counterparts further south. Colours follow the same trend of simplicity and directness.

One clue when trying to pinpoint a particular type of Caucasian rug or carpet is by examining the pile. If it is a rich, shaggy pile it is likely to have been woven in a mountainous district whose indigenous sheep are that much more hardy than their cousins in lowland areas and have thick long fleeces to protect them against the elements. Another tip is that mountainous tribes tended to use dense areas of hotter colours, reds, yellows, blues and occasionally greens. In the area by the Caspian Sea the carpets are smaller but the designs are more detailed and complicated.

Caucasian weavings fall into two distinct groups in terms of construction. The 'Kazak' group, which lies south of the Caucasus mountains (see map on page 150), includes the

Kazak, Lori-Pambak (detail), 1.3 x 2.3m (4'3" x 7'9"), c. 1850.

Kazak district itself, as well as the rug districts of Borjalou, Lori-Pambak, Talish, Karabagh, Chelabard, Karapchov, Lambalo, Karagashli, Genje, Shusha, Lenkoran and Moghan. Kazak rugs often have a fringe at one end only.

The other group is the 'Kuba', which lies north and east of the Caucasus mountains, and includes rugs from the Kuba district, as well as Seichur, Perepedil, Baku, Karagashli, Chichi, Surahani, Daghestan, Lesghistan, Shirvan, Marasali, Cheli and Derbend. Many Caucasian prayer rugs belong to the Kuba group, in which the weavers are almost exclusively Muslim, whereas rugs containing Christian symbols tend to be found among the large communities of Armenian Christians within the Kazak group.

Geometric designs

Kazak

The Kazak district is the largest weaving centre within the Kazak group, stretching from Erivan in Armenia in the south-western Caucasus, to Tiflis in the north and Karabagh in the south-east. The Kazak district produces both long-piled rugs from the mountainous areas and short-piled rugs from the lower regions. The simple, almost coarse, Kazak designs of angular medallions, multi-coloured octagons, lozenges and highly stylised rosettes have an appealing directness about them which no doubt explains their popularity with new tribal-carpet collectors. Likewise, the typically bold use of primary colours serves to heighten the impact of the overall look. Reds, blues, greens and yellows are the dominant colours. Particularly distinctive Kazak designs have acquired specific names. The 'sunburst' or 'eagle' design is the most instantly recognisable of all Caucasian carpet designs. The example shown opposite is a particularly powerful rendition of the two great outer wings guarding the central sunburst. The 'cloudband' Kazak

Talish, 1.1 x 2.1m
(3'6" x 7'), c. 1870.

is another distinctive design type, a motif that originated in China. The example shown on page 174 is a long-pile rug, and the field is scattered with an idiosyncratic variety of motifs, including horses and a man. The leaf-and-wine-glass main border is a typical feature of many Caucasian rugs, as are the two 'medecil' (interlocking) minor border designs.

Lori-Pambak rugs from the Kazak region display the characteristic Kazak stepped hooked polygon motif as well as massive geometrical medallions on a plain field (see illustration on the previous page). The piece shown once had a long pile which has now worn quite low, but the patina acquired through 120 years of use enhances the rich colours. It also has the typical Caucasian leaf-and-wine-glass border.

Talish

Talish is located in the south-eastern Caucasus and on the Caspian Sea. Finely woven using a soft lustrous wool, Talish carpets are long and narrow and have a distinctive design, often with plain fields which are usually blue, but can be red or green. Plain fields are highly sought after, but more often the fields are filled with rosettes, small squares or stars within squares. In the example shown left, particular emphasis is placed on the large flower-heads in the main border due to the plain nature of the field. Note the striking way in which the flowers close up together along the top and bottom borders.

Perepedil

Perepedil is located in the Kuba region. The substantial Muslim population here has produced a large number of prayer rugs, such as the example shown opposite. A typical Perepedil rug, this features the distinctive ram's horns device in the main field, as well as other symbolic shapes like scorpions. The border contains a kufic motif, which is a debased and decorative form of the Arabic Kufic script.

Floral designs

Karabagh

Karabagh is a mountainous area in the southern Caucasus. Antique examples dating from the late eighteenth century have a very strong French influence, with all-over floral

above: Perepedil prayer rug, 1.2 x 1.47m (3'10" x 4'10"), nineteenth century.

right: Karabagh, 1.5 x 5.5m (5' x 18'), c. 1880.

Kuba, 1.1 x 1.3m (3'5" x 4'4"), nineteenth century.

patterns of roses and flowers, paralleling the Russian court's obsession with all things French. This design influence continued well into the nineteenth century (see example illustrated), and is reminiscent of Savonnerie carpet design.

Kuba

Kuba, once a major rug weaving centre where some of the finest Caucasian rugs were made, is known for several different styles including typical Caucasian all-over patterns and the use of very attractive floral motifs stylised to the point of being almost geometric in appearance. The carefully drawn flowerbursts on the rug illustrated left are very dramatic against the blue-black background, and are endlessly repeating. The leaf-and-twig border is found in many Kuba rugs.

Baku

Baku is in the south-eastern Caucasus on the Caspian Sea, near the Persian border. Consequently designs are complex, like those of Persian rugs, and are finely executed with short pile.

The use of blue in a wide range of intensities is the dominant characteristic of Baku rugs, ranging from pale blue to the darkest turquoise, on a dark blue or black ground. The patterns are tightly disciplined with a pleasing rhythm about them; one of the most attractive is a field woven with polychrome botehs and serrated-edged octagons (see example shown opposite), though some designs have botehs only. Sometimes birds and animals are incorporated into borders. The barber's pole is often used as a border, as in the illustration. The long narrow format is typical of Baku rugs, as is the endless field of the central panel.

Seichur

Seichur is located within the Kuba region, near Derbend on the Caspian coast. Rugs from this area have a broad 'X' repeated down the field. They often show a clear European influence in their depiction of floral forms, seen in the example opposite in the vivid red cabbage roses that appear in the main border. The European influence was probably intended to appeal to the tastes of wealthy nineteenth-century Russians.

above: Baku Hila, 1.55 x 3.8m (5'1" x 12'5"), nineteenth century.

right: Seichur, 1.3 x 1.9m (4'3" x 6'5"), nineteenth century.

flatweaves

The term 'flatweave' is correctly used to describe a flatwoven as opposed to a pile carpet, that is, where the construction consists of only the warp and the weft without the addition of rows of knots, thereby creating a usually tightly woven flat surface. The correct terminology is 'slit-weave tapestry'. Flatweaves include kilims or kelims (the Persian term is 'gelim'), soumakhs, brocades and Indian dhurries.

It is an astonishing fact that kilims, now the most popular choice of flatweave for a furnishing carpet, were all but ignored as recently as the 1950s. It was only in the late 1960s and early 1970s that their potential was recognised by a handful of carpet experts, before and after which kilims were being ripped out of Turkish mosques, only to be replaced by fitted carpets. Today kilims are more popular than ever and are to be found in every style of interior all over the world, from Manhattan lofts to rural cottages and castles. Such is the vogue for kilims that many textile designers have drawn on their bold designs and striking colours as a source of inspiration for furnishing fabrics. It is a far cry from the beginning of this century when kilims were used to wrap pile carpets being exported to the West.

Woven for domestic use, kilims have been made for hundreds of years by nomadic tribes all over the Near East. The typical patterns and colours of the majority of kilims have an arresting direct appeal. They could not be further removed from the rarefied world of medieval Persian carpets, but in their own way they are just as pleasing to the eye. Their charm lies in the inherent sense of pattern and celebration of colour handed down through the generations in tribal weaving milieus. Each tribe and district has its own recognisable vocabulary of motifs and colours.

Persian kilims

The most striking feature of Persian kilims is their strong and clear colouring that makes them light-hearted, joyful and vibrant in character. A distinctive yellow colour is typical, as is a sharp white. Charming for their simplicity, they are visually uncomplicated, relying for effect on a wide variety of distinctive geometric designs within simple compositions. The strong geometric influence was introduced by people coming down from the Caucasus in the sixteenth century, as in the Kurdish kilim from Luristan illustrated, in its

above: Qashqai kilim, south-west Persia, 1.5 x 2.4m (5′ x 8′), nineteenth century.

right: Kurdish kilim, probably Luristan, central Persia, 1.69 x 3.3m (5′6″ x 11′), c. 1880.

Turkish kilim, possibly central area, 1.8 x 4.6m (6′ x 15′), c. 1850.

use of the six-sided lozenge which is found in Caucasian kilims. Another common design in Persian kilims is shown in the Qashqai kilim illustrated on the previous page, with its strong design motif of large diamond lozenges in the main field, and the dramatic 'medecil', or interlocking border, here in black and white. The ribbed borders at either end are also typical of Qashqai kilims.

Turkish kilims

Turkish kilims were produced throughout this vast country. One feature of Turkish life influenced the dimensions of their kilims, which was that the interiors of their houses were small and therefore looms were narrow. Kilims were often woven in two halves, or narrow border strips were added to increase the width of the kilim, as can be seen in the kilim shown here, which was made in three sections, where the joins are concealed in the white strips just inside the main border.

The three kilims illustrated demonstrate the range of style in Turkish kilims. The white ground example on this page is influenced by animal forms, as is common to many Turkish kilims – here in the form of scorpion tails in the hooked lozenges running down the centre. The use of white denotes a special-purpose rug used for weddings and other celebrations. The example from Konya shown opposite is a contemporary kilim which employs a design variant of a 'parmakli', or finger, design which is traditional to Turkey. The piece from central eastern Turkey employs the bold colours typical of this area, and is a small jewel-like rug with expanded flower-head designs in its central field. It was probably made to exhibit the skills of the weaver, possibly as a dowry rug.

Caucasian kilims

The Caucasus region consists of Georgia, Azerbaijan, north-east Turkey and north-west Iran. The coastal regions were heavily traversed by travellers following the silk route, but the interior was highly dangerous and rarely penetrated by travellers. This meant that the traditional carpet designs remained unchanged for centuries as weavers did not come into contact with outside influences.

The boldness of Caucasian flatweaves in both the rigidly controlled geometric patterns employed and the strong colour palettes have an obvious appeal. Northern flatweaves, which are generally referred to as Kuba kilims, use for the decoration of the

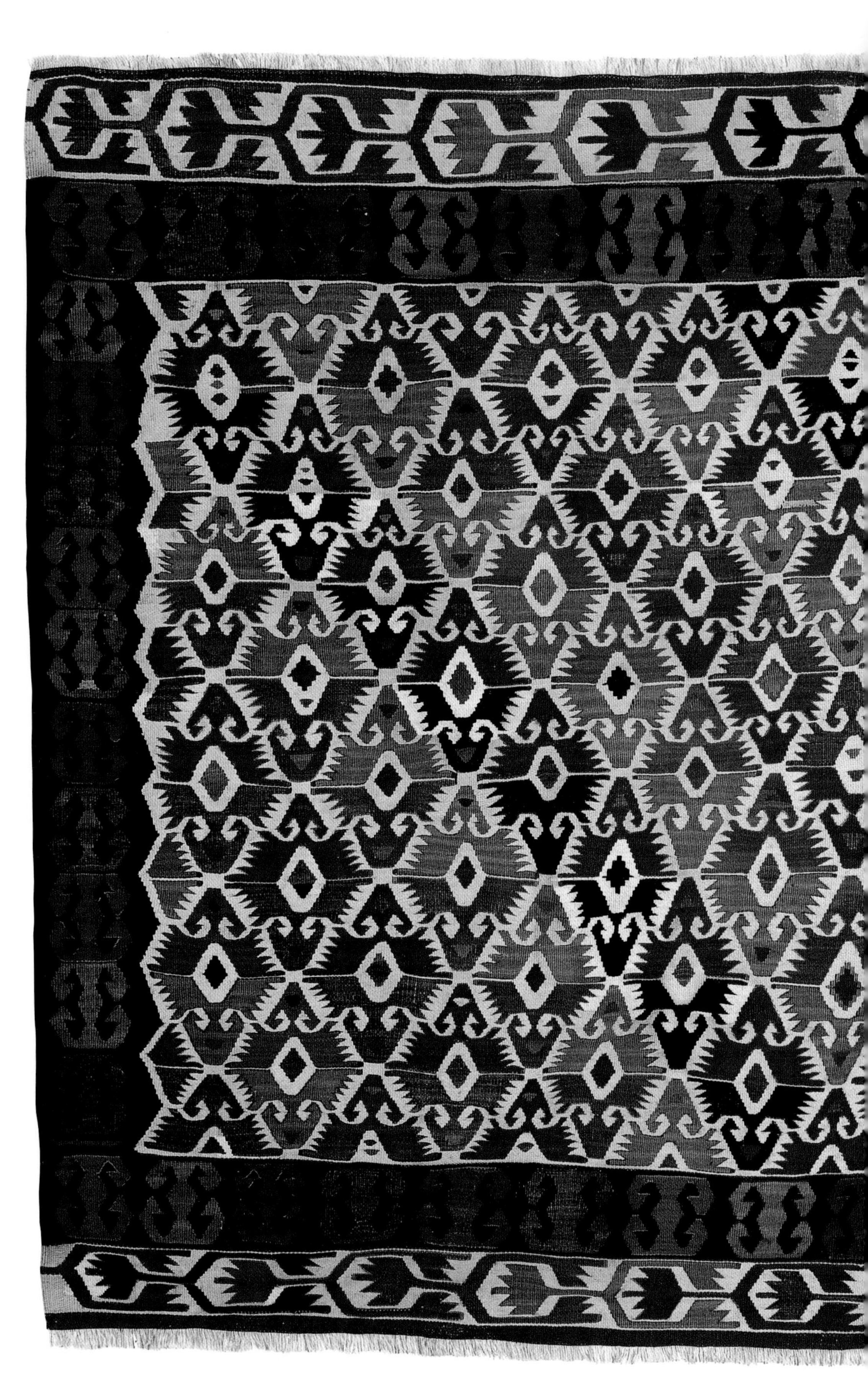

above: Turkish kilim, Konya, 1.5 x 1.8m (5′ x 6′), contemporary.

right: Turkish kilim (detail), central eastern area, 1 x 1.5m (3′6″ x 5′), c. 1860.

above: Shirvan Pallas kilim, Caucasus, 1.8 x 3.6m (6′ x 12′), nineteenth century.
right: Kuba kilim, Caucasus, 1.7 x 3.6m (5′6″ x 12′), nineteenth century.

Thracian kilim, 3.5 x 3.5m (12′ x 12′), nineteenth century.

field a repeat pattern of either stylised animal forms or geometric medallions reminiscent of Central Asian prototypes. The field is then framed by one or, more rarely, two narrow borders, usually with a continuous linear design and sometimes a repeating element. The Kuba kilim illustrated opposite employs the geometric medallions and vertical lines typical of kilims from this area, using colour to create a sense of variety in the repeating forms.

The southern or 'Shirvan' kilims rarely have borders and are characterised by a series of alternating wide and narrow bands containing rectilinear geometric designs such as composite hexagonal medallions, palmettes, diamonds, arrowheads and zigzags. The Shirvan kilim illustrated uses characteristic hooked medallions and has no border.

Thracian kilims

Thrace lies at the south-eastern tip of the Balkan peninsula. It consists of north-eastern Greece, southern Bulgaria and the European part of Turkey. Woven by people settled in villages and towns, Thracian kilims show a consummate mastery of the art of flatweaving, demonstrating that it is possible by bending and twisting their warps and their wefts to render curves in a variety of patterns. The designs have a strong marine atmosphere. Some feature stylised natural forms such as birds, plants and trees; others are composed of abstract geometric designs. All tend to have a field which contains a directional composition surrounded by a wide border which consists of either a repeat design, or a continuous floral pattern, or a combination of both of these.

The distinctive colour palette widely employed of a blueish-green, deep wine red and dark blue is easy to recognise. The example illustrated features tiny mihrabs, or prayer arch forms, as a design feature in the border, and as a main mihrab in the field. The deep blue ground is reminiscent of the sea, and includes shoals of fish-like shapes, with the mihrab filled with seaweed and other underwater plants. Another colour combination sometimes encountered is chocolate brown with ochre yellows, light greens and blues. Thracian kilims are generally around 3.5 metres (12 feet) square and very occasionally a smaller format (0.9 x 1.6m / 3′ x 5′).

right: Balkan flatweave tapestry, 1.8 x 2.8m (6′ x 9′2″), nineteenth century.
opposite, above: Magri dhurrie (detail), 1.8 x 4.8m (6′ x 16′), late nineteenth century.
opposite, below: Jaipur dhurrie, 4.6 x 5.4m (15′4″ x 17′10″), nineteenth century.

Balkan flatweaves

Balkan, or Bessarabian, flatweaves employ a tapestry technique, and are more European in their curvilinear design vocabulary than the flatweaves from the main oriental weaving areas. The colours are typically pastels, as in the example illustrated opposite, although some striking examples use a black background.

Indian dhurries

Dhurries are flatwoven carpets that have been made in every part of India since at least the fifteenth century, and which underwent a revival in Indian prison workshops last century under British colonial rule. They are always made from cotton, a plentiful native resource (sheep do not thrive in the arid Indian climate, so there are few woollen rugs produced in India). Dhurries serve many purposes, from small personal bed dhurries, to long communal prayer carpets in mosques, and large special-purpose dhurries for celebrations, such as weddings, family gatherings and feasts. They were also used in the great palaces of maharajas, where they could reach up to 7.5 x 18m (25' x 60') in size.

Widely made for both local and export use, the most common design is one of simple stripes. The two examples illustrated show highly sophisticated designs and demonstrate the eclectic nature of the design influences from which the weavers draw: the Magri dhurrie, with its exotic palm leaf and floral designs in a riot of reds, greens and yellows, is an unusual and highly sophisticated example, and the Jaipur dhurrie design is based on Hispano-Moresque tiles.

turkoman

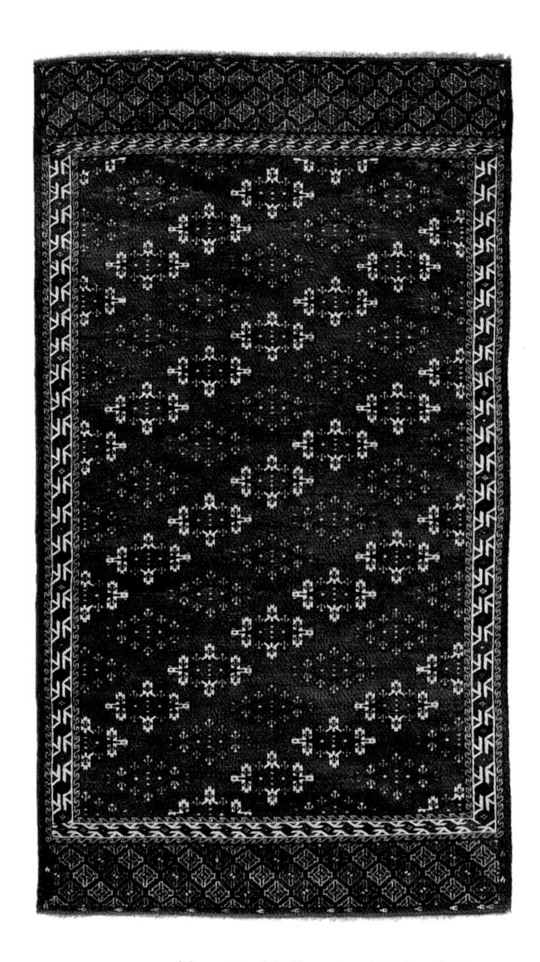

Yomut with Kepsi gul, 1.7 x 2.9m (5'6" x 9'7"), c. 1890.

Of all nomadic tribal weavings, those of the Turkomans are among the most distinctive, as well as being the most inventive. Believed to have come from the steppes of Asia at least two thousand years ago, the Turkoman traversed a vast area stretching from the Caspian Sea in the west to Tibet in the east, bounded north and south by the borderlands of Russia and Persia. Today the principal Turkoman tribes of Yomut, Tekke, Ersari, Saryk, Salor, Chodor, Arabatchi and Kizil Ayak inhabit the area bound by the Caspian Sea and the Amu Darya river in Central Asia.

Each Turkoman tribe had its own emblem known as a 'gul', an octagonally shaped motif employed on their carpets in an endless repeat pattern in vertical rows usually with off-set patterns of minor guls. If a tribe was defeated by another, or was assimilated into another tribe, its guls would be absorbed into the superior tribe's patterns, akin to the complex genealogical European tradition of armorial quarterings.

For the Turkoman, like all nomadic tribes, weaving was an integral part of their daily existence. Executed with great pride by the women, weaving was employed for everyday objects such as storage bags, saddle bags, tent strut covers and door rugs. One of the most easily recognisable characteristics of Turkoman weavings is that the ground colour, which is almost always a shade of red, remains the same in both the border and the field. The reds range in intensity from a purplish hue to a clear bright red.

The nineteenth-century Russian expansion into Central Asia was to have a significant effect on Turkoman weavings. Many of the Turkoman people were forcibly settled, becoming cotton farmers. At first the women weavers continued producing their traditional weavings which were eagerly sought after by carpet merchants buying for the European market. But commercialism soon led to synthetic dyes being used and the standardisation of motifs which hitherto had been the symbol of a particular tribe, now becoming the property of all. Regrettably the inherent purity of the ancient designs had become obscured by a desire to satisfy the western market. By the 1880s and 1890s, Turkoman weavings had become over-elaborate, the patterns were excessively detailed and crowded with ornament.

The examples illustrated are woven by three of the principal Turkoman tribes. The Yomut are the largest and most widely scattered of all Turkoman tribes. They use their tribal gul almost as a decorative pattern. Ersari carpets tend to use more curvilinear and freer designs than other Turkoman tribes, and in the example shown, yellow is used as

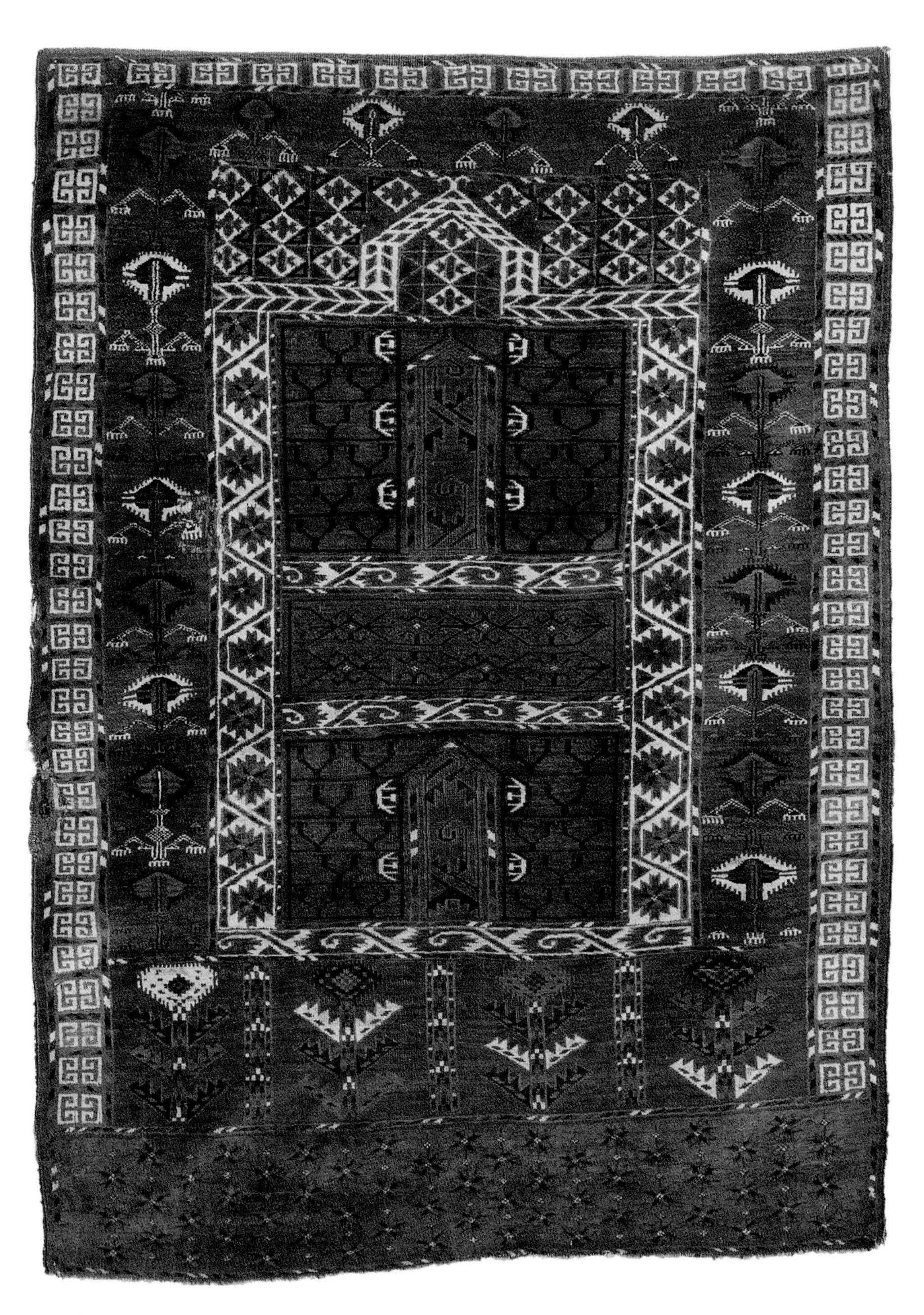

above: Ersari Beshir, 1.3 x 2.6m (4'3" x 8'6"), mid-nineteenth century.
right: Tekke engsi prayer rug, 1.15 x 1.5m (3'9" x 4'1"), end nineteenth century.

a framing colour. This large carpet was an 'audience carpet', used when great meetings of tribes assembled. The Tekke prayer rug illustrated was used as a door hanging, or 'engsi'. The square mihrab (prayer arch) is also found in other Turkoman weavings, but its decoration around the mihrab is unique to the Tekke prayer rug. The bottom skirt design is typically separated from the main body of the carpet in position and feeling.

east turkestan

East Turkestan is located in the middle of Central Asia, largely comprising the area occupied by the Takla Makan Desert. The only inhabited areas there are the oases on the desert borders, namely Kashgar, Turfan, Kucha and Aksu in the north, and Khotan, Yarkand, Keriya and Niya in the south. There are few carpets that can be accurately dated prior to 1800, and the best examples are from the nineteenth century, when they were produced for the export market. For many years they were called 'Samarkand' carpets, as this was the city in West Turkestan where they were sold for export.

Prior to the 1870s there was a tendency to make rugs using more vibrant and brighter colours than for those made after that date, when the use of chemical dyes and chemical washes was common to cater to the tastes of the western export market. There was a preference for the muted softer colours that chemical dyes produced. The three-medallion Khotan illustrated demonstrates this in its soft yellow ground and the washed-out pink of the three medallions and the border. Blues and yellows are very characteristic colours in East Turkestan carpets, used very effectively in the other example illustrated, which displays the strong colours that were typical before the chemical dyes were introduced.

The designs of East Turkestan carpets are highly distinctive and suggest a long established carpet tradition. The area was subject to a number of foreign rulers, and was thus influenced by many different styles which it absorbed into its own design culture. A common design is the pomegranate tree emerging from a vase, an ancient fertility symbol from the Far East. Another typical design features three round medallions in the field, probably of Buddhist origin, which symbolises the Buddha and his two acolytes. The first Turkic inhabitants would have brought such influences to the area. The medallion example illustrated is an unusual variant on this theme, as the two flanking medallions are square rather than circular. This rug also shows Chinese influences, in the fretwork in the outer border and in the two square medallions, in the single flower-heads on the pink ground in the border, and in the blue and yellow cloudbands in the central medallion. The other Khotan carpet also shows Chinese influences in its 'waves-of-the-sea' outer border and in the lotus flower-heads which fill the central field. The crowded combination of the field and border design containing ornamental elements is typical of mid-nineteenth-century East Turkestan production.

All East Turkestan carpets have a cotton foundation, with a lustrous woollen pile, which is soft and not very durable.

above: Khotan, 1.85 x 3.56m

(6′1″ x 11′8″), nineteenth century.

right: Khotan, 1.7 x 2.8m

(5′6″ x 9′3″), mid-nineteenth century.

china

above, top: Ningxia, 3.1 x 3.9m (10'2" x 12'9"), c. 1850. *below:* Mongolian carpet, northern China, 1.8 x 2.6m (5'10" x 8'5"), c. 1880.

It is little known outside the world of carpet experts quite how beautiful and sophisticated many Chinese carpets are. The popular image is one of mass-produced commercial carpets that are woefully bland in appearance with little aesthetic merit.

Chinese carpets have been woven since at least the Han and Tang dynasties (206BC–220AD and 618–906AD), but there are few extant examples dating from before the end of the seventeenth century. Early carpet weaving seems to have begun in regions such as Ningxia in north-western China, where the weavers were Muslim and therefore linked culturally to the East Turkestan carpet weaving tradition in Central Asia.

The majority of antique examples that survive were woven in the nineteenth century, probably for the western market. Traditionally carpets were a relatively minor art form in China and never achieved the status they were accorded in other parts of the Orient. Colour palettes tend to be sophisticated combinations of dark blues and camel or pale pinks, dark blue, terracotta and a subtle yellow. Patterns are tightly controlled in a carefully considered manner and, even if floral, have a restrained order. The use of geometric borders including a sort of Chinese version of the Greek key motif, or repeating swastikas offsetting motifs floating on the central field is typical. Many of the motifs have symbolic meaning, such as peonies which represent wealth and respectability.

Carpet production was mainly focused in northern China, although within that area it is difficult to attribute carpets precisely. Different types of Chinese carpet weaving can be identified. Ningxia was an important trading area and has a great reputation as a carpet weaving centre. Ningxia carpets are distinguished by their deep loose pile, supple texture and lustrous wool. They also have a cotton foundation with a woollen pile.The example shown is typical of Ningxia carpets in its use of blue and yellow, the pearl motifs in the inner border, and the Buddhist symbols in the main field. The Shou design carpet from Peking on the facing page shows another typical Chinese design motif in its use of Chinese symbols and fretwork.

The two carpets illustrated identified as Mongolian can only be speculative in attribution, as there is no firm evidence for carpet production from this area. The example with the butterfly and peony design is typical of the period around 1880, in its use of the ivory and two blues, and in its regimented use of the motifs. The plain Mongolian carpet with the open field and border is more unusual and is particularly striking in its modern simplicity of design.

above : Mongolian carpet with open field and border, 3.6 x 4.6m (11'9" x 15'3"), c. 1880.
right: Shou design carpet, Peking, northern China, 3 x 4.1m (9'9" x 13'5"), late nineteenth century.

india

above, top: Agra, 3.65 x 4.8m (12' x 15'9"), c. 1860. *below:* Amritsar carpet with the Shah Abbas design, northern India, 2.67 x 3.88m (8'9" x 12'9"), c. 1900.

The early history of pile carpet weaving in India is a fascinating instance of cross-cultural influences. It was probably Persian weavers from Herat in present-day Afghanistan who introduced the art of weaving pile carpets to India in the reign of the Mughal ruler Akbar (1556–1605), although flatwoven cotton dhurries have a much longer history in India (see 'Flatweaves'). Like the Safavid Dynasty in Persia, Akbar established workshops in several cities including Agra and Lahore for producing works of art. Indian Mughal carpets are amongst some of the most ravishing carpets ever woven. Gloriously coloured and often on a rich red ground, the carpets show a markedly strong Persian influence in the preference for floral patterns often in a lattice format, depicting flowers found in India such as the opium poppy, iris and hibiscus.

The majority of surviving Mughal carpets are floral in design, but a small group of naturalistic animal carpets are also extant. These appear fantastical to western eyes because of the inclusion of exotic Indian animals such as elephants, gazelles and cheetahs. Mughal carpets are extremely rare and expensive. The legacy of Mughal carpets lived on in subsequent Indian carpet design, however – these early carpets established a strong tradition of asymmetric positioning and an inventive use of open space to frame the different plant and figurative motifs which has continued in various manifestations and incorporated other influences, such as Persian designs, up until the present day.

Sadly the art was short-lived and by the end of the eighteenth century, Mughal influence had declined, along with the standard of carpet weaving, although some fine carpets do survive from the eighteenth and early nineteenth centuries. But it was not until the mid-nineteenth century under British colonial rule, after some fine Indian carpets were exhibited at the 1851 Great Exhibition in London, that western interest was sparked off and a revival of the weaving industry was encouraged. The main centres of weaving production were government workshops utilising the manpower of long-term prisoners in the country's jails, and commercial factories, which were set up at Agra, Amritsar, Srinagar and Mirzapur. They collected and copied old Indian carpets and invented new patterns based on traditional Indian designs, both in the Mughal and Indo-Isfahan styles, and also based some carpet designs directly on Persian models. Unfortunately, this revival was only partially successful due to the often poor quality of carpets that were produced. The good quality copies of Persian and Mughal carpets

A modern copy of a lattice with 'vine leaf' design Agra carpet (detail) by Kennedy Carpets, sizes range from 2.4 x 3m (8' x 10') to 3.6 x 4.5m (12' x 15').

from the second half of the nineteenth century, mostly made in prisons in limited numbers, are eagerly collected today.

It is also impossible to divide India into different weaving centres as one can in Turkey or Persia. The techniques do not vary greatly from region to region, as all Indian carpets are made in commercial and government workshops, and there is no tradition of tribal weaving.

Agra carpets have been very popular since the nineteenth century in Europe and America. The most famous nineteenth-century example was commissioned for Queen Victoria, to celebrate her appointment as Empress of India, when she received a 12 metre- (40 foot-) wide Agra carpet for the Waterloo Room in Windsor Castle, which is still in situ. The strongly curvilinear element of many Agra carpets imbues them with a sophisticated rhythmic quality and is to be found in both antique and contemporary examples. Many of the best examples were woven by prisoners in the jail workshops. Extremely decorative and often woven in sizes that are easy to accommodate in

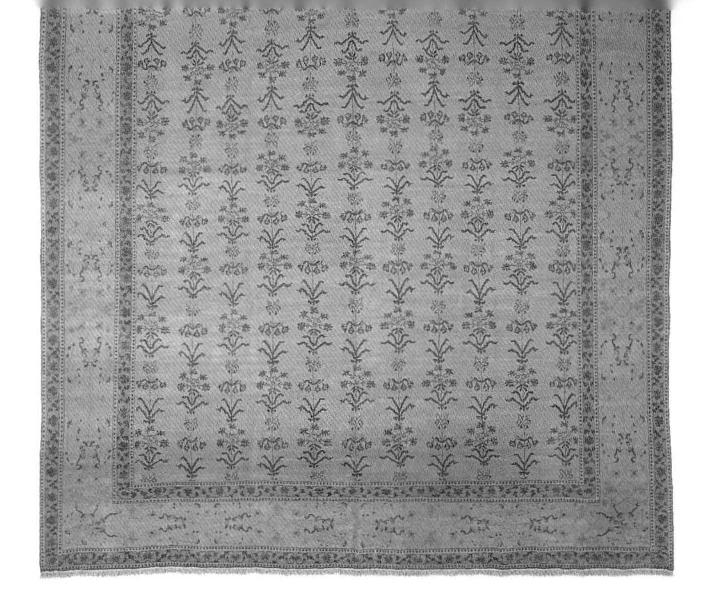

western interiors, Agras are very sought after by interior decorators. The nineteenth-century Agra carpet illustrated on page 194 is an unusual design but is still based on the concept of the Indo-Isfahan style, a typical Indian design, in its use of palmettes, flower-heads, curved cloudbands and feather-like leaves that resemble bat-wings in the main field. The quality of the piece is obvious in the glowing quality of the wool, the very thick pile and the richness of the colours.

The two modern Agras illustrated show how effective accurate reproductions of traditional designs can be at their best. These are made by Kennedy Carpets and are produced in India to a very high standard, and offer an opportunity to acquire faithful copies of Agras at an affordable price, in a range of colours and sizes. The lattice carpet with a 'vine leaf' design is copied from a late nineteenth-century example which can be related back to the floral carpets made in India and Persia during the seventeenth century, and the colouring is very similar to the original example. The 'shrub' carpet is based on a late nineteenth-century Agra jail carpet, which is of Mughal inspiration and was a popular design with Indian weavers of this period. The original Mughal shrub carpets were made for the ruler of Jaipur in the mid-seventeenth century. The colours of this reproduction have been altered but are still within the tradition for this type of Agra.

The Amritsar carpet shown on page 194 is also a jail carpet, and features Indo-Isfahan design elements in its palmettes and curved cloudbands. It is woven in pale, washed-out colours which were probably used to appeal to western tastes.

above, top: a modern copy of an Agra 'shrub' design carpet (detail) by Kennedy Carpets, sizes range from 2.4 x 3m (8' x 10') to 3.6 x 4.5m (12' x 15').

below: Indo-Persian, possibly Lahore, 4.26 x 7.6m (14' x 25'), early nineteenth century.

The early nineteenth-century Indo-Persian carpet shown left is also based on a sixteenth-century Isfahan design, with the characteristic feather-like leaves in the field and border, and palmettes and cloudbands covering most of the field.

Today India is one of the most important centres of weaving for the western export market, producing carpets in a multitude of styles from different cultures, even European copies. They are produced in several towns including Srinagar, Amritsar, Jaipur and Agra.

tibet

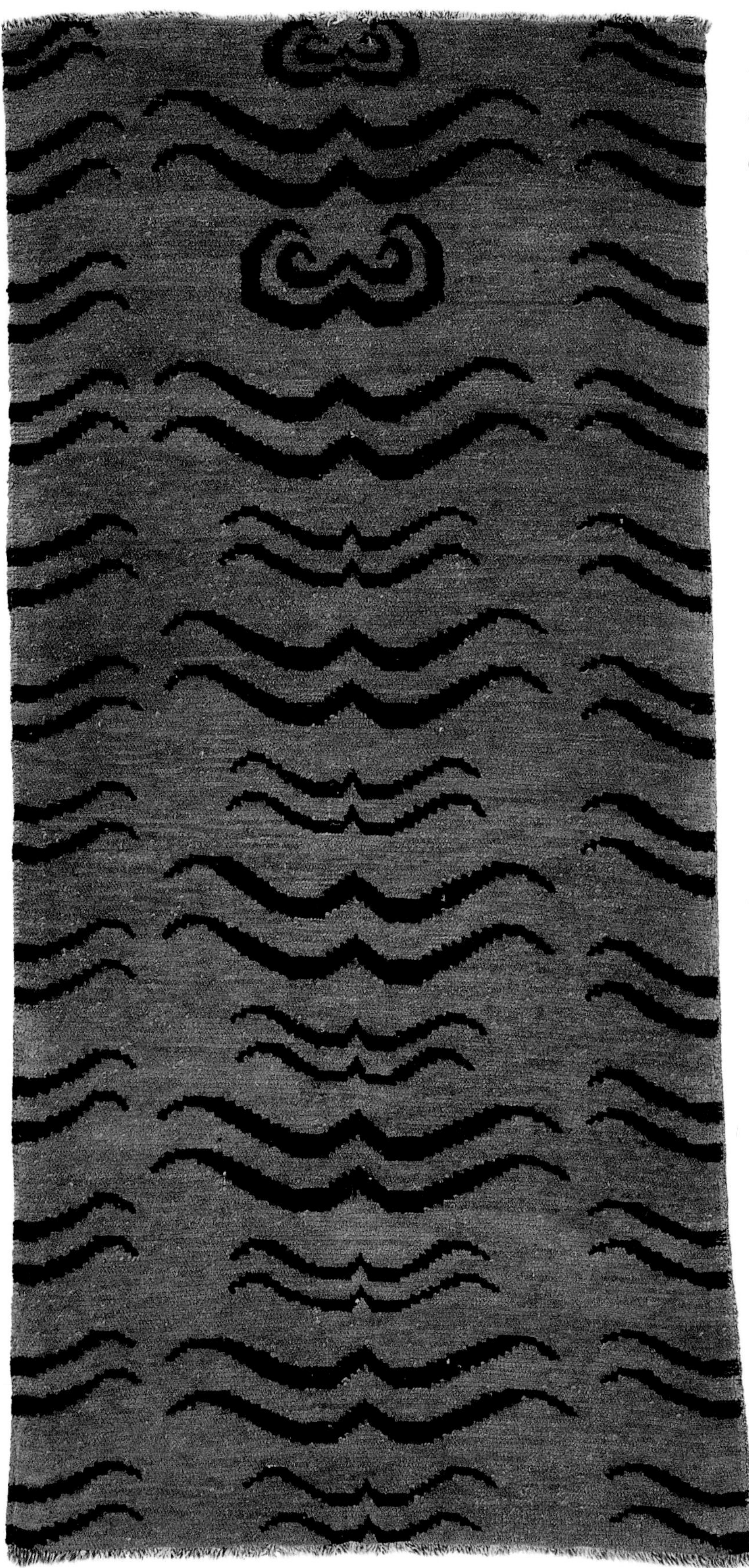

In all probability the history of weaving pile rugs in Tibet stretches back some nine hundred-odd years but there are few surviving examples dating from before the end of the nineteenth century.

The main distinguishing feature of all Tibetan rugs is the use of the cut-loop technique (curiously also found in Finland), which can encompass anything from two to five warp threads. Another characteristic is the thickness of the pile which can be as much as two centimetres (three-quarters of an inch). Rugs are usually, but not always, backed and bordered by a red cloth.

The designs are strongly influenced by Chinese and East Turkestan carpets, drawing heavily on Chinese iconography by often incorporating cranes, bats, lions, vases with flowers and dragons, sometimes paired with phoenixes. The borders are usually decorated with swastikas, T-shapes or naturalistically drawn flowers. A vibrant colour palette is very typical. Ground colours tend to be blue, black, red and orange and occasionally yellow and ivory. Tiger rugs, such as the example shown, are a very distinctive Tibetan design and are popular in Europe and America.

Today carpet production in Tibet is limited, but the tradition is continued by refugees based in Nepal and India, who often weave carpets specifically for the western market.

Tiger rug, 0.82 x 1.73m (2'8" x 5'7"), c. 1880.

europe & america

France

The early history of carpets in France is in essence the story of the two weaving ateliers, Savonnerie and Aubusson. There are earlier references to carpets being woven in France before the seventeenth century, but no examples survive. Henri IV of France's granting of a licence in 1608 to Pierre Dupont to manufacture Savonnerie carpets is similar in spirit to the establishment of court workshops by the Mughals and Safavids, whose common aim was to produce superlative works of art, including carpets.

In 1627 Louis XIII gave a royal 'privilege' to Dupont (1577–1640) and his pupil Simon Lourdet (d.1671) for weaving carpets. They set up business in an old soap factory, hence the name **Savonnerie**, which quickly became the label attached to the products of the factory – carpets, panels and wall hangings – all created exclusively for the court. From the beginning, individual designers were employed to create designs, all of which were totally European in style. Unlike early American or British carpets, no attempt seems to have been made by the Savonnerie atelier to emulate oriental carpets. A law was passed to prohibit the importation of carpets from the East to France in order to safeguard the Savonnerie workshop, which was granted a monopoly for the weaving of knotted-pile carpets.

The seventeenth-century Savonnerie carpets have an opulent grandeur about them, no doubt explained by the close links between the factory and the court. Until 1768 the factory worked chiefly, if not exclusively, for the court, producing pile carpets only. The richness of the colours used and the supremely confident manner with which acanthus scrolls, classical motifs and floral motifs were handled, combined to create a sumptuous effect worthy of any royal household. In 1663 Colbert, one of Louis XIV's ministers, stipulated that a painter from the Royal Academy had to oversee the designs for the carpets and to teach the drawing to the staff every month. Several important painters were associated with Savonnerie in this way, notably Charles le Brun and, later in the eighteenth century, François Boucher.

Stringent State economies due to the financial problems arising from the wars in the latter part of Louis XIV's reign were largely responsible for the decline of the factory between 1690 and 1712. However it was later revived and produced very pretty feminine carpets akin to the prevailing styles in the other decorative arts of the era. Soft colours, delicately drawn flowers, floral swags and ribbons are typical. But its heyday

Savonnerie in the Louis XV style, 5 x 3.6m (16′4″ x 11′10″), c. 1840.

was over and by the beginning of the nineteenth century, cheaper Aubusson carpets were more popular, although Napoleon later employed the factory to weave handsome Empire-style carpets. In 1825 Savonnerie was amalgamated with the Gobelins tapestry factory and its independent existence came to an end.

The example illustrated is an 1840 copy of a Louis XV design, and is probably quite true to the original colours. The pile is typically lustrous, as are the classical scrolls and floral motifs.

Aubusson was best known as an important tapestry-weaving centre until the King's Council set up a carpet-weaving enterprise there in the early 1740s, in an attempt to meet the great demand for knotted carpets. Flatwoven carpets were not introduced until the late eighteenth century. To begin with, the carpets were copies of imported Turkish examples. Louis XV and Madame de Pompadour were among the first clients placing orders through agents in Paris. But the demand for oriental carpets did not last, and the artist Pierre-Josse Perrot, who had already been involved with designing Savonnerie carpets, was called upon to design carpets in the French style in 1750. Another painter, Le Lorrain, produced a radical new design, 'a grande mosaique', which was a sophisticated precursor of the nineteenth-century floral carpets. A central medallion of flowers is surrounded by dainty rosettes, flowers and garlands. The example illustrated left shows a 'First Empire' carpet with a beautifully drawn Empire design of a central medallion and small flower-heads in the field, in vibrant colours with an unusual white ground border. The green background field colour is typical, as is a tobacco brown.

Aubusson carpets were originally made as both knotted-pile carpets and, later in the eighteenth century, as flatwoven slit-tapestry technique carpets produced in the same way as their tapestries. The Aubussons that are popular and readily available today are flatweaves.

The Aubusson floral tradition was never completely abandoned, although the vogue for the neo-classical Empire style, which was created

by two architects (Percier and Fontaine) after the Proclamation of the Empire in 1804, gave rise to some very handsome Savonnerie and Aubusson carpets whose patterns are strongly influenced by the antique, often incorporating classical trophies or Etruscan and Roman motifs. These tend to be in a darker richer palette, sometimes in different shades of the same colour, resulting in an almost 3D-look.

Nineteenth-century Aubusson tapestry-woven carpets, which were produced in great quantities, are popular with interior decorators in Europe and America today. Trailing ribbons, bows and blowsy roses woven in soft pastel shades – rose pinks, dove-greys, café-au-lait, and pale yellows – make for an ultra-feminine look which is very suited to sophisticated drawing rooms. The two examples of nineteenth-century pieces illustrated are both in soft colours. The Louis Philippe period carpet is wool and silk on a cotton foundation and uses a very delicate design of flowers and foliage with a central medallion and arabesque scrolls in the field and border, all of which are typical of that period. The Napoleon III example above uses a characteristic late nineteenth-century plum colour, and is a simpler design with a slightly coarser weave.

opposite, top: Louis Philippe period Aubusson, 5.7 x 4.6m (18'7" x 15'2"), c. 1840.

opposite, below: 'First Empire' Aubusson, 4.8 x 3.9m (15'9" x 12'8"), c. 1800.

above: Napoleon III Aubusson, 2.85 x 1.9m (9'4" x 6'5"), c. 1880.

Aubussons are not very durable and well-worn Aubusson carpets tend to disintegrate. Any fragments salvaged are usually re-used for upholstery or cushions.

Seventeenth- and eighteenth-century Savonnerie and Aubusson carpets are extremely rare and consequently very expensive. Examples can be seen in national museums and historic houses open to the public. There are, however, several companies producing good-quality reproductions (see the International Directory).

England

The early history of carpet production in the British Isles is dominated by attempts to imitate oriental-style knotted-pile carpets. Very little tangible evidence survives, but it is believed that the art was introduced to Britain by Flemish weavers escaping religious persecution in the Low Countries in the sixteenth century. The second Earl of Ormonde and Ossory in Kildare, Ireland, established a short-lived carpet weaving business using Flemish weavers in the early sixteenth century.

The earliest surviving example of a knotted-pile English carpet is a 5.8 metre- (19 foot-) long carpet dated 1570, incorporating heraldic devices within its blue, yellow and green floral design, originally commissioned by John Harbottel of Crowfield, Suffolk. It seems likely that the carpet was made by Flemish weavers who had settled in East Anglia.

Such was the popularity of oriental carpets that it was not until the eighteenth century that a carpet industry in Britain was properly established. During the first half of the eighteenth century, there was a great vogue for highly decorative floral needlework carpets. Feminine and highly decorative, they were largely embroidered by the ladies of the household, drawing on pattern books. By 1775, the dawning of neo-classicism coupled with the revival of knotted carpet weaving in Britain put a stop to such pretty designs.

Still exclusively the preserve of the luxury market, hand-knotted-pile carpets from 1761 until the end of that century were produced either by Thomas Moore's factory at Moorfields or Thomas Whitty's factory at Axminster. A major advantage that both these companies had over oriental carpet producers was their ability to make knotted-pile carpets to exactly the size required. Many late eighteenth-century carpets were specially commissioned to echo features of the interiors for which they were intended. This practice helps to explain the unity of so many

opposite: Moorfields carpet designed by Robert Adam, 4 x 1.7m (13′ x 5′6″), late eighteenth century.
above: Axminster, 5.5 x 3.65m (18′ x 12′), c. 1800.

neo-classical ensembles. Robert Adam's great neo-classically inspired carpet designs were designed to reflect the ceiling of the room for which they were commissioned, and both Moore and Whitty produced carpets for him. The Adam carpet produced by Moorfields illustrated is typical in its neo-classical style. There is a similar carpet in the Red Drawing Room at Syon House in London. Adam borrowed liberally from contemporary publications of engravings of the many ancient ruins being discovered during the period he was designing carpets. For example, a carpet at Osterley Park, Middlesex, is clearly inspired by the coffered soffit of the Temple of the Sun at Palmyra, Syria. The Axminster carpet shown is unusual in having a green field rather than the more common brown. It is less common for Axminsters to have an overall floral pattern, as the designs are usually more formalised with medallions, in a similar style to Savonnerie carpets. This informal design is more suited to English tastes.

During the early nineteenth century, the designs of knotted carpets became more diverse, ranging from florid rococo revival examples to 'Turkish' patterns, which were popular for masculine rooms such as libraries or dining-rooms.

In the mid-nineteenth century, the British carpet industry underwent a dramatic revolution as steam-powered looms replaced the old hand-looms. Concurrently the standard of designs being produced drastically deteriorated as the manufacturers endeavoured to appeal to the common denominator of taste.

Arts and Crafts carpets embrace a wide variety of carpets which do not have a strong common thread, other than the fact that they grew out of a desire by a handful of influential artists, designers and architects, to promote sound principles of design. With hindsight it was a predictable reaction in an age when technological advances had led to larger markets with less cultivated tastes than ever before.

The key figure when discussing the evolution of the Arts and Crafts movement is William Morris. He was instrumental in showing that it was possible to produce beautiful hand-knotted carpets in the West that were not merely debased oriental designs churned out in carpet factories. He did, however, draw heavily on Persian motifs, along with seventeenth-century Italian textiles and Chinese art for inspiration in his carpet design. His first carpets were shown in his Morris and Co. London shop in 1880. In due course, Henry Dearle (1860–1932) took over the design of the carpets woven first in Hammersmith, London, and later at Merton Abbey and then Wilton. One of his carpets,

above, top: William Morris 'Hammersmith' studio carpet, designed by Henry Dearle, 3.5 x 4.6m (11'6 x 15'), c. 1890s. *below:* 'Hammersmith', a modern adaptation of the carpet illustrated above, by Asia Minor Carpets, made to any size.

the 'Hammersmith', is illustrated left. A modern reproduction of this same design is also shown, made by Asia Minor Carpets of New York, which demonstrates that good quality copies of Arts and Crafts carpets are available today at a more affordable price than the originals, which now command very high prices. The stems of the flowers in Dearle's carpet tend to be broad and the different elements of the design stand independently: one can easily distinguish the palmettes or flower-heads.

Carpets of the Arts and Crafts movement were never made in great numbers. Only a discerning few recognised their quality at the time. As John Aldam Heaton, writing with harsh realism in the 'Art Journal' in 1889 estimated, 'as for the trade in goods of the character of Mr Morris's productions, probably it does not altogether amount to one-fourth of the business done by one firm in Tottenham Court Road alone'.

The leading manufacturer of Arts and Crafts carpets was Alexander Morton. In what must have at the time seemed a foolhardy enterprise, he set up a carpet weaving workshop in County Donegal in Ireland. He enlisted the help of weavers from the Wilton carpet factory to teach hand-knotting to two women at the Morton factory at Darvel, Scotland, who then went to Donegal to teach the Irish girls. The designs produced were very varied, as were the colour palettes. It was a period that coincided with a Celtic revival in Ireland and, by 1901, Morton was busy producing carpets with Celtic designs, drawing for inspiration among other sources on a recent reprinting of the seventh-century Book of Kells. The results were enthusiastically received and it was not long before Liberty of London mounted an Irish carpet exhibition in 1903. The accompanying leaflet states: 'The charm of these carpets is...they have an artistic quality of individuality which no power loom can give'. Donegal carpets were exported to America where many were sold in the New York showrooms of Gustav Stickley and their use advocated in his influential magazine 'The Craftsman'.

Highly decorative, Donegal carpets encompass a wide variety of designs, including several patterns loosely based on stylised plants and flowers, twisting and curling in a rhythmic fashion, such as the 'Glenmure piece' illustrated opposite, attributed to Voysey. It was described in the Liberty catalogue of 1903 as 'a treatment of teazel and leaves', suggesting a Gothic influence, with a border of similar ornament. Some Donegal carpets are clearly inspired by oriental carpets, whilst others are an attractive mixture of ancient Celtic decorative motifs given an Art Nouveau twist.

'Glenmure' Donegal carpet designed by C.F.A. Voysey, 3.65 x 4.9m (12' x 16'), 1903.

Individual one-off commissions were an important aspect of the Donegal workshop output. R.S. Brinton writing in 'Carpets' published in London in 1919, mentions the main European centres for the manufacture of hand-knotted carpets, and includes the Morton Donegal company: 'Their staple trade has always lain rather along the lines of specialities. They have catered rather for architects, decorators, individuals or public bodies, who were inspired by some particular idea, and who could afford to pay for it, than for the ordinary customer'.

At the time, manufacturers and retailers such as Liberty were keen to exploit the new style, and many leading designers of the Arts and Crafts movement were commissioned to draw up carpet designs as the vogue gradually spread, including the Scotttish architect and designer George Walton (1867–1933), Walter Crane (1845–1915), Mackay Hugh Baillie Scott (1865–1945), C.F.A. Voysey (1857–1941) and Frank Brangwyn (1867–1956). However, there is little common visual identity in any of the designs and they were manufactured using various techniques: some of them were hand-knotted, some hand-woven and some machine-woven.

America

It was only the very wealthy who could afford to import carpets and rugs in the early days of colonial America. The majority of the population made do with either bare boards sprinkled with sand or floors covered with a mixture of ox blood, clay and sand which was impacted on the floor before being given a good polish.

By 1850, however, Andrew Jackson Downing observed that 'the floors of the better cottages in this country – at least, in the Northern States, are universally covered with carpet or matting'. The carpets Downing refers to are probably **hooked rugs**. Although there is evidence that hooked rugs were made in many other countries including Scotland and Finland, today they are generally associated with America and, along with patchwork quilts, have become an icon of American folk art.

The first hooked rugs were made by housewives using simple home-drawn patterns. Marked out on burlap (hessian), they were easy for one worker to take over from another at a rug-hooking bee. The range of patterns varied from simple geometric designs to naive images of animals and flowers. Like many indigenous art forms, certain designs are linked with one particular area. For example, block patterns and basket weave appears in mats made in New Brunswick, Canada. Eighteenth-century examples are very rare, and the majority of antique examples that survive date from around 1840 to 1900. They are still made today as a form of elevated craft on both sides of the Atlantic (see the Contemporary section of Carpet Types for modern productions).

The method of making hooked rugs is extremely simple: worked from the top, strands of rags (early examples used wool, later cotton was used), are pulled through a material with a loose weave such as linen or burlap. On completion the loops are sometimes cut to create a textured pile. In the late nineteenth century, pre-stamped patterns on burlap were manufactured by enterprising designers such as Edward Sands Frost of Biddeford, Maine, who was in-

Hooked rug, derived from Edward Sands Frost pattern, 0.84 x 1.52m (2'9" x 5'), late nineteenth century.

Third Phase Chief Blanket, 1.5 x 1.9m (5′ x 6′2″), c. 1846.

valided out of the Army and became a pedlar. The hooked rug illustrated, a well-executed design of a lion with rope and leaf border, is almost certainly derived from one of his patterns. Small in size, hooked rugs tend to be oblong, but are sometimes also oval or round in shape.

Navajo rugs, originally woven as blankets by eighteenth-century Navajo Indians, are the American equivalent of tribal rugs. The bold geometric patterns in an equally strong colour palette are very distinctive and have become a symbol of the American West.

It is generally believed that the Navajo learnt the art of weaving from the Pueblo Indians around 1700. Originally the Navajo wove the rugs to be used as blankets. The Pueblo Indians used cotton, but began to use wool following the introduction of sheep by the Spanish into the South West in the early seventeenth century. They employed a type of tapestry weave which is characterised by their technique of slatting or stepping the edges of the motifs to avoid making slits.

Navajo rugs are often brilliantly coloured, frequently employing a strong red known as 'Bayeta' red, as well as blacks, greens, whites and yellows. The rug shown is an example of the finely woven Chief Blankets. It is one of the Third Phase Chief Blankets, characterised by the diamond motifs appearing out of the stripes, which are surrounded by a border of eight triangular elements .

The advent of the railroad, the establishment of trading posts by white traders and the curiosity of the early tourists in the South West around 1870 all combined to have a dramatic effect on the Navajo weavers, who suddenly found themselves busy churning out blankets which were used as rugs by the new market. Synthetic dyes and ready-to-weave yarns were used and inevitably the quality declined. Fortunately a couple of enlightened traders including Lorenzo Hubbell in the late nineteenth century recognised the need to preserve the traditional methods. His trading post in Arizona is now a National Historic Site and has a good collection of painted sketches of chiefs' blankets and other traditional patterns.

Antique examples of Navajo rugs are highly sought after, especially in America and are very expensive. Poor quality copies are made today.

Art Deco

In the 1920s and 1930s there was a great vogue for abstract Art Deco-style carpets designed by artists, architects and designers in Europe and America. The stylistic term 'Art Deco' arose out of the International Exhibition of Modern Decorative and Industrial Art in Paris in 1925. The geometric-patterned carpets that were included in interiors at the exhibition were to have an enormous impact on international carpet design (see Ruhlmann interior on page 28).

below, top: Wool carpet by Jacques-Emile Ruhlmann, 2.24 x 3m (7'4 x 9'10"), c. 1925. *bottom:* Wilton hand-knotted wool carpet by Edward McKnight Kauffer, c. 1929.

It is possible to distinguish between two main types of Art Deco carpet design in the period either side of the momentous 1925 Paris exhibition. The first is that which adheres more closely to the traditions of carpet design in France, its essential components being an elegance of line and strength of underlying form often enhanced with linear 'caprice' or floral exuberance. Edouard Bénédictus's carpet of 1925 illustrated here is typical of this style, in its extravagant use of swags and garlands in rich colours, which are anchored by the trellis pattern to the purple field. The carpet also exemplifies much of the work being produced by designers for the relatively new 'ateliers' of the grand Parisian department stores, such as La Maitrise of Galerie Lafayette, established in 1920, and the integrated decorating firms such as the Compagnie des Arts Français set up by André Sue and Louis Mare in 1919, and that of one of the most outstanding decorators of his time, Jacques-Emile Ruhlmann. The Ruhlmann carpet illustrated is typical in its stylised, non-figurative patterning in rich shades of burgundy, pink and beige.

The second type of Art Deco carpet design was inspired by the innovations in painting begun some fifteen years earlier by the Cubist painters. The artists Férnand Léger and Sonia Delaunay were thus inspired in their carpet design, and the latter explored her colour theories to dramatic effect throughout the 1920s. Ivan da Silva Bruhns was another prominent figure and one of the few artists to successfully explore the ultimate fusion of new pictorial ideals with the practical necessities of weaving (see an example of his work on page 29). The startlingly abstract results gained increasing popularity throughout Europe in the 1920s and 1930s as artist/architect designers such as Eileen Gray, Marion Dorn and her husband

Floral carpet by Edouard Bénédictus 2.2 x 3m (7'4 x 9'10"), c. 1925.

Edward McKnight Kauffer (see illustration) and Betty Joel in turn embraced the design challenge that carpets presented. Nowhere is this better illustrated than in the work for the great ocean liners, from the 'Normandie' to the 'Orion', for which Jacques-Emile Ruhlmann, Eileen Gray and Marion Dorn among others were commissioned to design carpets. The new technology demanded a new look and this was perfectly engendered in the work of these designers.

Art Deco carpets are highly sought after today, and as decorative pieces, they look very much at home in modern interiors, as the abstraction of their design is so much a part of today's interior style. Pieces by the top designers are very expensive, but the lesser-known pieces are still fairly affordable.

contemporary

Over the last few years there has been a remarkable surge of interest in interiors. This has had a beneficial effect on many aspects of interior design and the decorative arts, including carpet design. Not since the 1920s and 1930s has there been such a choice of contemporary rugs available on both sides of the Atlantic. The variety of styles available to the potential rug-buyer is vast, and the selection included here is just a sample of the best designs currently available. Further details of other designers are detailed in the International Directory at the back of the book. This chapter includes top-quality 'designer carpets', which combine the talents of designers from many different fields – fine art, fashion, textile design – with the traditional craftsmanship of carpet dyers and weavers, to produce carpets of great and lasting artistic value; modern 'rustic'-style carpets, based on artisan-produced carpets, such as Swedish Larsson-style cotton runners or the charming simplicity of American hooked rugs; and modern adaptations of oriental rug styles such as yataks, or gabbehs, and tulas, made using traditional techniques but with modern abstract designs and fashionable colours.

Designer carpets

This area of contemporary carpet design has produced some exciting talents in recent years. **Helen Yardley** is perhaps best known for her collections of inexpensive abstract woollen rugs. Her rugs are hand-tufted and broadloom, and she finds inspiration from diverse sources, including Henri Matisse, Robert Motherwell, Roger Hilton and Isamu Noguchi.

The rugs by American **Judy Ross** are hand-woven or hand-stitched in India. Her various sources of inspiration include Eileen Gray and the painter Sonia Delaunay. Many of her designs are one-off commissions.

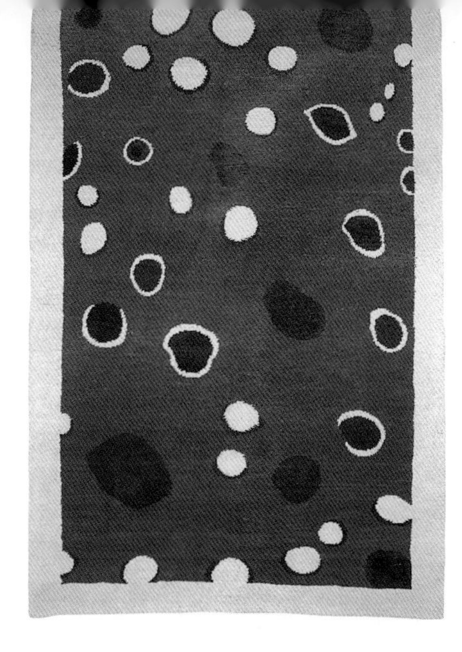

opposite, top: 'Adore' by Helen Yardley, 1.82 x 2.74m (6' x 8'10"); *middle:* runner by Helen Yardley, 0.8 x 3.8m (2'7" x 12'6"); *below:* 'Zig Zag' by Judy Ross for Salon Moderne, in any size or colour; *above, top:* 'Leopard Cowrie' by Veedon Fleece, in any size or colour; *below:* 'Zebra' from Veedon Fleece, 1.2 x 2.1m (4' x 6'9"); *right:* Sandy Jones pile carpet, 3.2 x 3.5m (10'6" x 11'6").

Veedon Fleece was set up in 1992 by Adam Gilchrist, who had previously worked in the carpet department of Sotheby's auction house in London. As well as producing one-off commissioned carpets, Veedon Fleece has its own collection of designs which is wide-ranging in scope and includes such designs as a reproduction of a C.F.A. Voysey carpet, a modern chequerboard-style carpet and a Tibetan tiger rug. The carpets are hand-knotted in Nepal using wool from the Tibetan mountains and can be woven up to very large sizes (24 x 10m/80' x 33'). Tibetan Thangka artists paint the designs by hand.

Designer **Sandy Jones** has had a long and varied career working with textiles, first in the fashion industry, and then as a costume designer, before setting up her own studio to design carpets and textiles in 1990. She was commissioned by the rug designer Christopher Farr to design a limited-edition collection of rugs which were exhibited at the Royal College of Art, London, in 1994. Sandy Jones's designs exhibit a quiet confidence often using only two colours to great effect. Fascinated by texture, her love of 'abrash' (change of colour tone caused by dye variations) imbues her carpets with discreet shifts of colour tone.

One of the most influential forces in carpet design today is the British designer **Christopher Farr**. Originally an artist by training, he dealt in oriental rugs before turning to designing and commissioning contemporary carpets. In 1988, his first range of carpets was launched. Since then, he has worked with a diverse selection of painters, such as Bill Jacklin and Royal Academician Gillian Ayres; and fashion luminaries including Romeo Gigli, Rifat Ozbek and Georgina von Etzdorf, and textile designers. The rugs are made using traditional methods and materials, and are hand-knotted in Konya in central Turkey.

British-born **Christine Vanderhurd**, based in New York, is well known in America for her exuberant and often vividly coloured designs. Enormously diverse in style, many of her designs show the influence of her original career as a textile designer working in fashion and home furnishings for firms such as Mary Quant, Biba, Liberty and Osborne & Little. Vanderhurd uses several different techniques including needlepoint, over-tufted machine-made broadloom as well as hand-tufting.

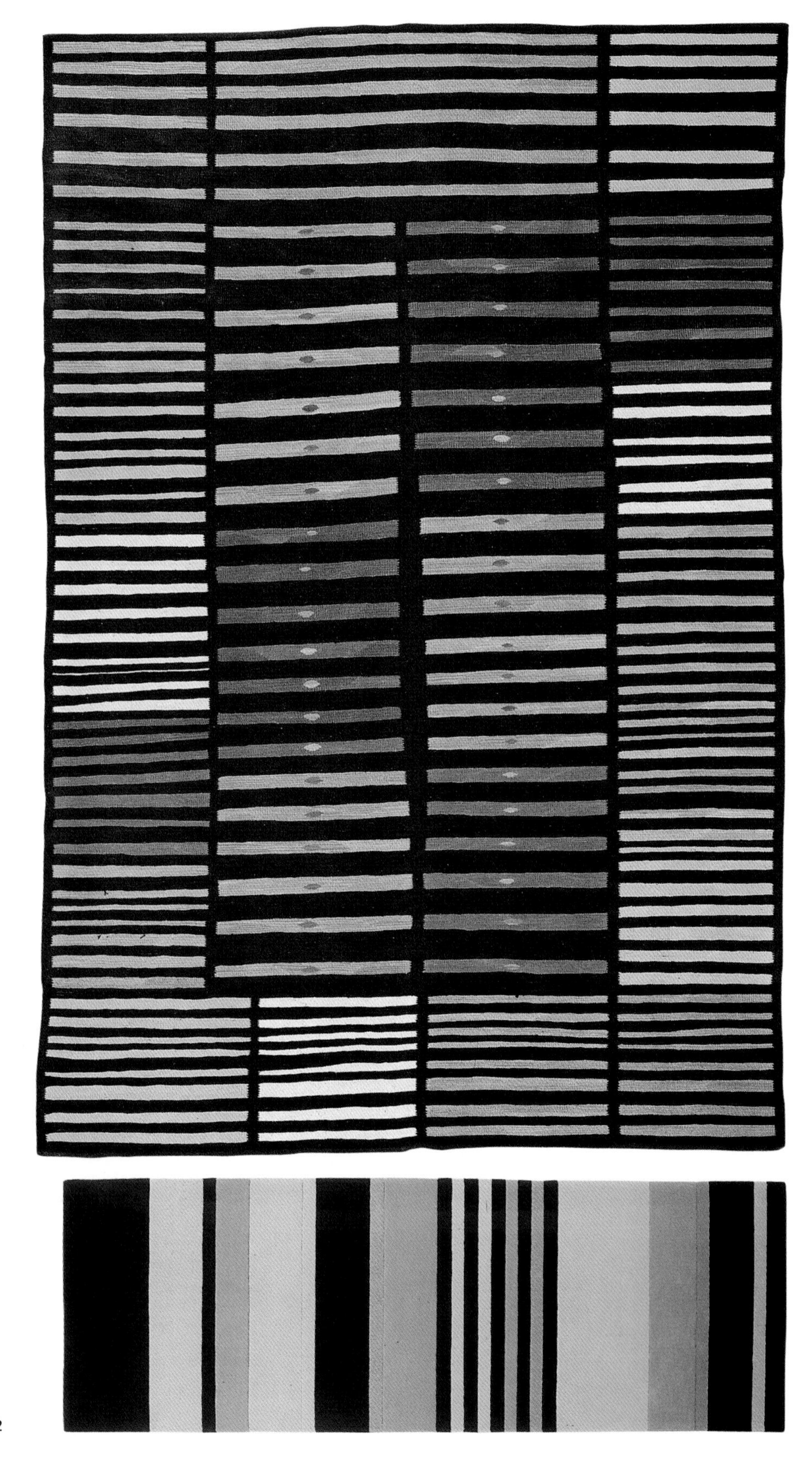

Modern rustic carpets

opposite, clockwise from top left: 'Colourwoven' flatweave designed by Georgina von Etzdorf for Christopher Farr, 1.8 x 2.75m (5'10" x 9'); 'Atlas' flatweave (detail) by Christopher Farr, 1.8 x 2.75m (5'10" x 9'); 'Skydive' pile carpet designed by Georgina von Etzdorf for Christopher Farr, 1.8 x 2.75m (5'10" x 9'); 'Tra La La Night' by Christine Vanderhurd, 1.5 x 2m (4'6" x 6'9"); 'Monticello' by Christine Vanderhurd, available in any size.

right: Two Swedish runners from Nordic Style, based on original eighteenth-century Swedish designs, woven in India.

The recent vogue for pared-down interiors is a look that embraces various different rustic styles, including Swedish and Shaker. It appears effortlessly simple, but is in fact carefully contrived, with a few well-chosen objects such as cotton Swedish runners or American hooked rugs. Such rugs were originally woven by artisans. Modern reproductions are either hand- or machine-woven and can look very effective in the right setting. It is their naive charm that is so beguiling.

The Swedish look should more correctly be termed Gustavian as it takes its inspiration from the neo-classical genre that became popular during the reign of Gustav II (1771–1792), and has become very popular through magazines such as 'The World of Interiors' and 'House Beautiful'. The main elements are light colours, simplicity and an understated elegance. The uncluttered interiors typically feature pale floorboards and painted furniture with injections of colour from checked or patterned curtains, slip covers and cotton runners. These elements are greatly to contemporary tastes. Faithful copies of eighteenth-century style cotton **Swedish runners** are readily available on

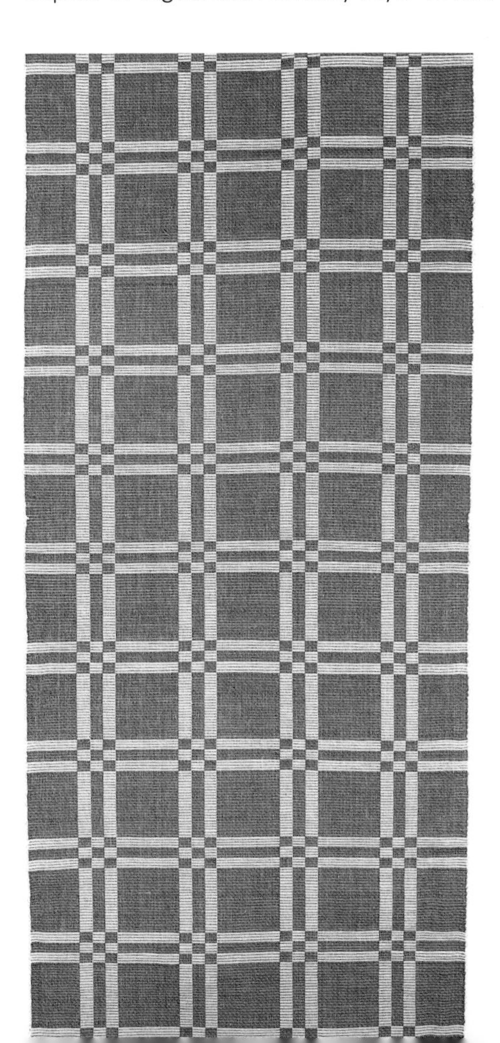

both sides of the Atlantic from companies such as the London-based **Nordic Style**. This particular firm produces runners which are sold off the roll to the length required, and can either be used as runners or stitched together to form carpets. Typical colourways, in the classic Swedish tradition, are blue and white, green and white, red and white, and beige and white.

In keeping with the search for an idealised homespun lifestyle, **hooked rugs** are enjoying a welcome revival of interest. America is the country with which the hooked-rug tradition is most commonly associated, and the American designer **Claire Murray** is a leading light in this field, producing hooked rugs in the traditional American style. Her work has a charming naive quality and is clearly influenced by the seaside culture of her Nantucket home. Her wide range of designs include many with a piscatorial theme, shells, several winsome depictions of many types of dogs and native American wildflowers, as well as several floral themes inspired by her own garden, which are based on nosegay bouquets – floral circular rings around a single blossom or cluster of flowers. The influences on her designs are wide-ranging, as can be seen in the examples illustrated: the 'Daisy' carpet is inspired by the floral textiles of William Morris, and the floral compartment rug by the Royal Botanic Gardens at Kew in London.

above, top: 'Daisy', by Claire Murray, 1.8 x 2.75m (6' x 9'). *bottom:* Hand-hooked rug by Claire Murray, 0.93 x 1.9m (3'1" x 4'9").

Oriental modernist carpets

The increasing popularity of contemporary oriental carpets which use traditional techniques and materials but are modernist and graphic in design has produced some very effective results. Two such examples are modern yataks, or gabbehs, and modern tulus, both of which are traditional techniques but have been adapted in their design or colour, or both, to suit modern tastes.

Yatak or **gabbeh** is a term used loosely to cover a wide range of thick-pile, coarsely

woven carpets made of wool and sometimes goats' hair. Yatak is the Turkish term, and gabbeh is the Persian name. They are more commonly known as gabbehs in the West. In Persia, they were originally made by tribal nomads in the Fars province of southern Persia, which is where the best examples are still made today. The typical colours are bright indigo blue, madder red and different tones of natural wool. They often exploit the attractive 'abrash' effect of using a single colour over a large area, where the dye variation produces an interesting subtlety of tones. They are extremely hardwearing. The two examples shown were made in Turkey for **Woven Legends**, a company based in Philadelphia. The three-medallion piece is an updated traditional yatak design. The yatak with the elongated central medallion and diagonal sprays is a modern design.

Tulu carpets are another deep-piled, wonderfully tactile type of oriental carpet which are currently enjoying popularity. They are woven with hand-spun angora goat hair which produces their characteristic soft lustrous pile. Woven in western Turkey, tulus are notable for their bold geometric designs, which are appropriate to their very coarse weave – more complex patterns would be hard to achieve. Exciting colourways are being produced for the contemporary market, usually in two colours only. The chequerboard design tulu shown was produced by **Woven Legends**.

above: Two modern yatak rugs made by Woven Legends; *top:* 1.2 x 2.1m (3'9" x 7'3"); *below:* 1.15 x 2.2m (4' x 7').

right: Modern tulu rug made by Woven Legends, 1.15 x 2.2m (3'9" x 7'3").

care & repair

To own a good carpet is a responsibility. A modicum of common sense and the following of a few basic rules are all that is required to give a carpet the care that it deserves. There is something inherently wilful about allowing a carpet to deteriorate. The ownership of works of art is akin to being a custodian for one's lifetime.
If considerable thought and money have gone into the purchase of a carpet the chances are that it will be cherished. On the other hand, inherited carpets tend to get rather a raw deal, often getting taken for granted and subject to the vagaries of small children and rumbustious dogs.

The first consideration having purchased a carpet is where it is going to be displayed. Is it going to be subject to strong sunlight, is it going to be walked over incessantly, is it to be used as wall hanging, or draped across a table, are chairs going to be dragged across it and so on. All of these are important factors which must be taken into account. Too much sunlight over any length of time will inevitably fade chemical and natural dyes with irretrievable results. Fading as a result of sunlight is a gradual process and it is usually too late to do anything about it by the time one becomes aware of what has happened. If the wear and tear of human feet can have a detrimental effect on a carpet it does not take much imagination to realise what effect heavy furniture or dining-room chairs frequently being pushed in and out can have. The solution to this widespread problem is to place the legs of furniture, particularly those with metal castors, on small glass discs thus protecting the pile. A good underlay is a prerequisite: not only does it reduce wear by taking up the unevenness of the floor, it also stops any movement on bare floors. Very few underlays on the market are effective. The most successful are made in Germany by Fulde Stop. One is thin and slightly adhesive on both sides and is best suited to lightweight carpets, holding them on all types of flooring, it is also suitable for fitted carpets. The other is thicker and relies on the weight of the carpet to stay in place. Fulde Stop is available from the better carpet shops.

Another commonly encountered problem is the curling of selvedges and corners. This is caused by extra tension being placed on the outer warps during the weaving and can be rectified by sewing cotton or jute webbing under the selvedges. A more long-term solution is to use a competent restorer to sew the edges flat by inserting extra weft threads which straighten out the curling edges.

If the carpet in question is too fragile or rare to be used as a floor covering, a good way of displaying it is to treat it as a picture and hang it on the wall. For hanging stronger carpets velcro-mesh is advisable. Two-inch (five centimetre) wide velcro can take the weight of a large and heavy carpet. It is wise to ensure that the carpet is hanging with the warp vertical and the pile lying downwards, the warp taking the weight. The velcro is tacked onto a flat length of wood which is fixed to the wall.

The sixteenth- and seventeenth-century fashion for carpets being draped over tables deserves to be more widely employed. Visually it is extremely effective and is an excellent way of using a carpet in slightly ropey condition that might not stand up to heavy foot traffic. Silk carpets not robust enough to hang by their own weight should be mounted on a frame like a painting.

cleaning

Needless to say there are all sorts of myths about how carpets should be cleaned. If in any doubt it is always worth asking a reputable dealer for advice, no matter how trivial your question may seem. All dealers can offer a specialist cleaning service, and will also advise on the cost of the work before proceeding. Dry-cleaning is detrimental to wool carpets as the chemicals remove too much of the natural oil from the fibres. It is best to wash them in relatively cool softened or deionised water with a mild liquid soap and leave them to dry of their own accord. On the other hand it is always advisable to have silk carpets dry-cleaned. But this should only be undertaken with the advice of an expert carpet cleaner.

It is safe to vacuum carpets, as long as one is not too rough. Fragile carpets should be vacuumed with a small dustette Hoover with a nylon net fixed over the opening. Beware of vacuums with beaters as they are potentially damaging. If a carpet is sent to a specialist cleaner, he will beat it to dislodge dirt and dust before embarking on the cleaning. This is done by slowly turning the carpet over and over in a huge drum. Inevitably in a family house there is bound to be the odd accident involving beverages or animal pets. Put a thick white towel under the wet area and dose it with water, having first ensured that the dyes are fast. This is done by dabbing each area of colour one by one with a piece of cotton wool. If any colour transfers on to the cotton wool the colours will run: seek expert advice. If the colours are fast the carpet should then be left to dry in its own good time, lifted off the floor so that air can pass beneath it.

repairs

Repairs are a highly emotive area. To many people a worn carpet coupled with a bit of fading has the appeal of faded grandeur. But if the life of a damaged carpet is to be extended, repairs are necessary, taking into account the value of the carpet in question. Obviously there are occasions when a carpet is too far gone to warrant an extensive outlay on repairs. Then there is the eternal debate between 'restoration' and 'conservation'. 'Restoration' will involve re-weaving and re-knotting; conservation is more a question of mounting the carpet onto a backing if it is particularly fragile, thus preventing the damage from getting worse. There are a handful of specialist firms that can be trusted (see the International Directory on pages 220–222).

storage
Never store a carpet that is damp or dirty. It may seem sensible to roll a knotted carpet with the pile inside, but it is potentially damaging to the foundation weave and furthermore is liable to damage the pile. Plastic or polythene should never be used to wrap a carpet in because they can trap moisture. To prepare a carpet for storage it should be wrapped in acid-free tissue paper on both sides before being rolled in a white cotton or linen cloth (cotton and linen are distasteful to moths and most insects). A carpet should be stored in a dry place with plenty of moth repellent such as strong herbs like cedarwood and should be inspected every three months or so. Do not trust removal companies to store carpets.

glossary

abrash
A word of Turkish origin meaning dappled, speckled or mottled, more commonly used to describe the appearance of a horse. In carpet lore it is applicable to the variations of density in colour in a single carpet caused by the vagaries of several batches of wool being dyed at different times resulting in an aesthetically pleasing subtle range of tones. This is most pronounced when one can clearly see where one batch of wool finishes and another starts: a distinct horizontal line is visible. A characteristic of nomadic or village weaving.

aniline *see* chemical dyes

arabesque
Intricate and fanciful interlaced and intricate decoration based on rhythmic linear patterns of scrolling and interlacing foliage, tendrils derived from Saracenic ornament or Arab designs. The origin of arabesques is disputed.

Ardebil
The superb 'Ardebil Carpet' was made c. 1530s in Persia and is believed to have come from the shrine of Sheikh Safi, at Ardebil. It was under the Safi dynasty (1499–1722) that Persian carpet weaving reached its zenith in the sixteenth century. The Ardebil is probably one of the most celebrated carpets in the western world and has been in the collection of the Victoria & Albert Museum since the end of the nineteenth century.

barber's pole
Multi-coloured diagonally striped border pattern found in Persian carpets and particularly in Caucasian carpets.

boteh
A single unfolding seed-shaped motif with a curving top like a pear at its narrowest point, more commonly recognised in Europe as the Paisley motif. It originated in the seventeenth century, evolving out of Persian and Indian flowering plant motifs. A more angular form can be found in Persian, Caucasian and occasionally Turkish carpets.

cartouche
Enclosed ornament repeated throughout a border, and sometimes in the field.

chemical wash
Washes of chemical compounds are used to give carpets an instant patina of age. A side effect is to weaken the structure of the carpet and make the pile brittle.

chemical dyes
Chemical dyes (also called aniline dyes) first introduced in the 1860s, were rapidly taken up and by the 1880s were ubiquitous in the Middle East. Made from coal tar derivatives the dyes are fugitive and fade to unappealing murky colours. They were banned for health reasons but their use continued and many people died.

chrome dyes
Fast synthetic dyes first used earlier this century which resulted in flat crude colours. In recent years the dyes have become much more refined.

chufti *see* jufti

cloudband
A stylised motif based on clouds of Chinese origin found adorning carpets in Anatolia, Central Asia, Persia and China.

cochineal *see* vegetable dyes

dhurrie
Indian flatweave carpets. Akin to kilims, the crucial difference being that they are cotton not woollen.

dosar
A Persian term for a small rug.

elephant's foot
Trade description of Turkoman 'gul' pattern.

field
The central part of a carpet contained within the borders.

guard stripe
A narrow stripe between borders, or between border and field.

gul
Lozenge-shaped motifs (guls) usually arranged in vertical rows typical of Turkoman rugs. Different variations can be ascribed to specific tribes as heraldic emblems similar to the family crests of European nobility.

Herati
Also known as the 'mahi' or fish pattern, the Herati design takes it name from the town of Herat (originally in Persia, now in Afghanistan). It consists of a lozenge of stems terminating in flower-heads surrounding a central rosette, with four lanceolate leaves curving symmetrically between the flower-heads. Widely used, there are numerous variations of the Herati design.

Holbein carpets
Term used to describe fifteenth-century Turkish geometric-patterned carpets that often appear in paintings by Hans Holbein (1497/8–1543). Lozenges and octagons are typical motifs often with kufesque borders. *See* kufesque; Lotto carpets.

indigo *see* vegetable dyes

jufti
Also chufti, djufti. A 'false knot' that is tied over four or more warp threads as opposed to the more customary two warp threads.

kilim
Also known as kelim (Turkish form), gelim, gilim, gileem (Persian forms). Term used to describe a pileless flatweave carpet in which the pattern is formed by the wefts which hide the warps.

khelleh
Long narrow carpets, but wider than runners (5m x 2m).

knots (see illustration on page 153)
Pile carpets are created by weavers knotting short lengths of woollen yarn around one or more (usually two) warp strands so that the ends of the yarns protrude to form the pile. The structure is secured by tying a knot to hold each individual yarn in place, a transverse row at a time. Knot counts vary from region to region as do the type of knots commonly used. The two most frequently encountered knots are: the Persian knot, also known as the Senneh, open or asymmetrical knot; and the Turkish knot, also known as the Ghiordes, closed or symmetrical knot.

The Persian or asymmetrical knot wraps around only one warp and results in a finer and tighter weave which is typical of Persian court carpets, almost all urban workshop carpets and some Persian village carpets. It is also found in India, Turkestan, Turkey, Egypt and China. The knot is described as being open to the left or to the right depending on which warp is wrapped.

The symmetrical knot is used mainly in Turkey, the Caucasus and Turkestan in both antique and modern carpets. It used to be known as the 'Turkish' or 'Ghiordes' knot because it is used in Persian carpets made by many tribes with Turkish or Kurdish ancestry. It is also found in European carpets. The cut ends of the knot project in the centre of the two warps around which it has been tied.

kufesque
The use of stylised Arabic Kufic script, often in the borders of carpets.

lac *see* vegetable dyes

Lotto carpets
A type of Turkish carpet seen in two paintings by the Italian artist, Lorenzo Lotto (1480–1556). Probably from the Ushak region, the carpets have a red background with yellow lattice-work contained within either a kufesque or a cartouche border.

madder *see* vegetable dyes

medallion
A decorative motif typically used in the centre of a carpet's field as the dominant element.

mihrab
The prayer arch or niche, orientated towards Mecca. Always found on prayer rugs.

mina khani
A repeating floral lattice stemmed pattern of large flower-heads each with small white flowers set in a diamond around it.

mordant
Metal hydroxides used to fix the colour. Iron mordants can be corrosive. Different mordants produce different shades and hues from the same dye.

pallas
Caucasian name for a flatweave.

palmette
Stylised motif derived from the lotus flower.

pine cone pattern *see* boteh

quatrefoil
Medallion with four rounded lobed sections.

runner
Term used to describe long narrow rugs.

running dog
Hooked border motif typical of Caucasian and some Anatolian carpets.

saf, saph
A prayer rug with a horizontal row of prayer niches, flat or pile woven.

selvedge, selvage
The long side of a rug's outer warps, which are woven as a rigid braided edge.

soumak, sumak
A type of flatweave using a floating weft.

spandrel
An approximately triangular space bounded by the outer curve of an arch and the enclosed mouldings.

synthetic dyes *see* chemical dyes

vegetable dyes
Otherwise known as natural dyes, used from ancient times to dye cotton and wool intended for weaving into carpets until the advent of chemical dyes in the mid-nineteenth century. For much of the twentieth century chemical dyes have been commonplace, but the subtle hues produced by vegetable dyes are beginning to be recognised and reintroduced.
cochineal: red dye obtained from the crushed and pounded bodies of insects.
indigo: a blue dye obtained from the crushed leaves of the indigo plant. Made synthetically c. 1890.
madder: dye taken from the roots of the madder plant 'Rubia tinctorum' which is prevalent throughout the Middle East. The colours include a deep-red brown, pinks, reds, oranges and purples.

warp
The vertical threads of a carpet's foundation. Before weaving can begin, the warp threads are strung on the empty loom to provide the framework for weaving. The fringes along the top and bottom of a carpet are the ends of the warp.

weft
The horizontal thread woven into the warp by being passed over and under the warp at right angles.

further reading

Oriental Rugs: A Buyers Guide, by Lee Allane, Thames & Hudson, 1992

The Country Life Book of Rugs & Carpets of the World, edited by Ian Bennett, Country Life Books, 1981

The Undiscovered Kilim, by David Black and Clive Loveless, published by David Black Oriental Carpets, 1977

World Rugs & Carpets: A comprehensive guide to the design, provenance and buying of carpets, edited by David Black, Country Life Books, 1985 (also published as *The Macmillan Atlas of Rugs and Carpets of the World*, edited by David Black, Macmillan Publishing Company, New York, 1985)

The Caucasus: Traditions in Weaving, by James D. Burns, Court Street Press, Seattle, 1987

The Unappreciated Dhurrie: A Study of the Traditional Flatwoven Carpets of India, by Steven Cohen, edited by David Black and Clive Loveless, published by David Black Oriental Carpets,1982

Oriental Rugs in the Metropolitan Museum of Art, by M. Dimand and J. Mailey, Metropolitan Museum of Art, New York, 1973

Oriental Rugs: A complete guide, by Murray L. Eiland Jr. and Murray Eiland III, Laurence King, 1998 (also published as *Oriental Carpets: A complete guide,* by Murray L. Eiland Jr. and Murray Eiland III, Bulfinch Press, 1998)

Country House Floors 1660–1850, by Christopher Gilbert, James Lomax, Anthony Wells-Cole, catalogue to an exhibition held at Temple Newsam House, Leeds 1987, published by Leeds City Art Gallery

Oriental Carpets: Philadelphia Museum of Art, by Charles Grant Ellis, The Herbert Press, 1988

Hali: The International Magazine of Antique Carpet and Textile Art, Hali Publications Limited, London

Arts & Crafts Carpets, by Malcolm Haslam, published by David Black Oriental Carpets, 1991

Tribal Rugs: Nomadic and Village Weavings from the Near East and Central Asia, by James Opie, Laurence King, 1992 (also published as *Tribal Rugs,* by James Opie, Portland, 1992)

Carpet and Textile Patterns, by Nicholas Purdon, Laurence King, 1996

Carpets and Rugs of Europe and America, by Sarah B. Sherrill, Abbeville Press, 1996

Silk, Carpets and The Silk Road, by Jon Thompson, published by NKH Culture Centre, Tokyo, 1988

Carpets from the Tents, Cottages and Workshops of Asia, by Jon Thompson, Barrie & Jenkins, 1983 (also published as *Oriental Carpets: From the Tents, Cottages and Workshops of Asia*, by Jon Thompson, E.P. Dutton, New York, 1983)

Rugs and Carpets from Central Asia, by Elena Tzareva, Penguin, 1984

Flowers Underfoot: Indian Carpets of the Mughal Era, by Daniel Walker, catalogue to an exhibition held at the Metropolitan Museum of Art, New York, 1998, distributed by Harry N. Abrams

international directory

The companies listed below are a selection of recommended dealers worldwide. Many of them take international orders and have a mail-order service – please contact them directly for further information.

Denmark

June Hilton
Design Works, Soender Boulevard 53, 4, 1720 Copenhagen V Tel. 45 31 31 90 87
Contemporary rug designer.

France

Maison Bakerdjian
10 rue Choron, 75009 Paris
Tel. 01 48 78 93 39
Antique and decorative oriental carpets.
Camoin-Demachy Antiquities
9 Quai Voltaire, 75007 Paris
Tel. 01 42 61 82 06 Fax 01 42 61 24 09
European carpets from the eighteenth to the twentieth century.
La Galerie Chevalier
17 Quai Voltaire, 75007 Paris
Tel. 01 42 60 72 68
Oriental carpets and European tapestries, especially Aubussons.
Robert Four
8 rue des Saints-Peres (corner of rue de Vemeuil), 75007 Paris
Tel. 01 40 20 44 96
Antique Aubussons and Savonnerie carpets.
Nicole Mainguet
'Soleil d'Orient', 2 rue Tranchee des Gras, B.P. 211, 63006 Clermont-Ferrand Cedex 1, Nice Tel. 04 93 8 82 04
Antique oriental carpets.
Jean Maniglier
89–95 rue de la Monnaie, Bp 119, 59009 Lille Tel. 03 20 13 05 05
Contemporary carpets and rugs.
L'Ourartien
19 rue de L'Odeon, 75006 Paris
Tel. 01 46 33 07 57
Kilims and some tribal carpets.
Suzanne Sadaule
3 rue Alphonse-Karr, 06000 Nice
Tel. 04 93 87 82 04 Antique oriental, Chinese and Russian carpets.
Galerie Triff
35 rue Jacob, 75006 Paris
Tel. 01 42 60 22 60 Fax 01 42 60 39 94
New and antique kilims, gabbehs and modern Iranian carpets.

Germany

Franz Bausback
Teppichantiquitäten, Kunstrasse, N3, 9, D-68161 Mannheim Tel. 0621 12 92 80 Fax 0621 10 59 57 Oriental carpets.
Galerie Azadi
Deichstrasse 24, 20459 Hamburg
Tel. 040 36 36 20 Fax 040 37 12 08
Antique carpets and textiles.
Krausse
Maximilianplatz 15, 80333 Munich
Tel. 089 29 48 91 Fax 089 29 89 38
Antique carpets.

Great Britain & Ireland

A.D. Carpets
227 Westbourne Grove, London W11 2SE
Tel./Fax 0171 243 2264
Antique oriental carpets.
Anglo-Persian Carpet Company
6 South Kensington Arcade, London SW7 2NA Tel. 0171 589 5457
Antique oriental carpets.
The Asad Company Ltd
5 Earls Walk, London W8 6EP
Tel. 0171 937 0415 Fax 0171 937 5417
Made-to-measure carpets and kilims; traditional and contemporary designs.
Atlantic Bay Carpets
5 Sedley Place, London W1R 1HH
Tel. 0171 355 3301 Antique oriental carpets.
David Black
96 Portland Road, London W11 4LN
Tel. 0171 727 2566 Fax 0171 229 4599
Antique and contemporary oriental and European carpets using natural dyes. New carpets and dhurries can be made to order.
Frank Bolger Oriental Rugs
58 Maddox Street, London W1R 9PA
Tel. 0171 629 7825 Fax 0171 495 6127
Antique oriental and European carpets.
The Edinburgh Tapestry Company
Dovecot Studios, 2 Dovecot Road, Edinburgh EH12 7LE Tel. 0131 334 4118
Contemporary rugs, many by leading artists.
John Eskenazi (see also Italy)
15 Old Bond Street, London W1X 4JL
Tel. 0171 409 3001 Fax 0171 629 2146
Antique rugs and textiles; oriental art.
Fairman
218 Westbourne Grove, London W11 2RH
Tel. 0171 229 2262 Fax 0171 229 2263
Mostly modern oriental rugs.
Christopher Farr
115 Regents Park Road, London NW1 8UR Tel. 0171 916 7690
& 212 Westbourne Grove, London W11 2RH
Tel. 0171 792 5761 Large range of contemporary carpets by top designers.
S. Franses
80 Jermyn Street, London SW1Y 6JD
Tel. 0171 976 1234
Antique oriental and European carpets.
Victoria Harley
Tel. 0171 371 3836
Consultant in nineteenth-century and earlier oriental and European carpets.
Alastair Hull
The Old Mill, Haddenham, Ely, Cambs CB6 3TA Tel. 01353 740 577
Fax 01353 740 688 Kilims, especially from Central Asia, Iran and Afghanistan.
C. John
70 South Audley Street, Mayfair, London W1Y 5FE
Tel. 0171 493 5288 Fax 0171 409 7030
Carpets, rugs, tapestries and textiles; cleaning and restoration.
Sandy Jones
Chester Jones, 240 Battersea Park Road, London SW11 4NG
Tel. 0171 498 2717 Fax 0171 498 7312
Contemporary rug design. By appointment.
Kennedy Carpets
Oriental Carpet Centre, Building G, 105 Eade Road, London N4 1TJ
Tel. 0181 800 4455 Fax 0181 800 4466

Makers of high quality reproduction oriental rugs, especially Agras.

Keshishian Antique Carpets
73 Pimlico Road, London SW1W 8NE
Tel. 0171 730 8810
Antique oriental and European carpets.

The Kilim Warehouse
28a Picketts Street, London SW12 8QB
Tel. 0181 675 3122 Large range of kilims.

Peter Linden
15 George's Avenue, Blackrock, Co. Dublin, Republic of Ireland Tel. 3531 288 5875
Fax 3531 283 5616 Mostly antique oriental and European pieces but also stocks top-class contemporary rugs made with natural dyes. Also offers full restoration, washing and valuation service.

Clive Loveless
Tel. 0181 969 5831 Fax 0181 969 5292
Dealer and consultant in antique tribal rugs and textiles, specialising in Baluch, Kurdish, Cauasian rugs; early antique textiles from Ottoman Turkey; Central Asian suzanis and ikats and Moroccan and other African textiles.

Nordic Style
109 Lots Road, London SW10 0RN
Tel. 0171 351 1755 Fax 0171 351 4966
Swedish cotton runners, chenille rugs, painted floorclothes, as well as furniture and fabrics.

Roger Oates
The Long Barn, Eastnor, Ledbury, Herts HR8 1EL
Tel. 01531 632 718 Fax 01531 631 361
Contemporary rugs in natural materials such as wool, cotton and abaca (superior natural matting); some designs based on traditional country house-style Venetian runners.

Richard Purdon Antique Carpets
158 The Hill, Burford, Oxon OX18 4QY
Tel. 01993 823 777 Fax 01993 823 719
Antique oriental carpets.

Rau
36 Islington Green, London N1 8DU
Tel. 0171 359 5337 Fax 0171 209 4835
Carpets and textiles (including ikats), kilims, costume, jewellery and artefacts from Central Asia.

Rezai Persian Carpets
123 Portobello Road, London W11 2DY
Tel. 0171 221 5012 Fax 0171 229 6690
Antique Persian carpets, European textiles including Aubussons.

Clive Rogers
Postal address: P.O. Box 234, Staines TW19 5PE Address to visit (by appointment): Coach House Studios, 66 Staines Road, Wraysbury, Berks
Tel. 01784 481 177 Fax 01784 481 144
Antique, tribal, village and classical carpets and kilims; textiles and associated works of art; historical analysis and curatorial appraisal.

Sanaiy Carpets
57 Pimlico Road, London SW1W 8NE
Tel. 0171 730 4742 Fax 0171 259 9194
Antique oriental carpets including kilims, European tapestries including Aubussons.

Robert Stephenson
1 Elystan Street, Chelsea Green, London SW3 3NT Tel. 0171 225 2343
Decorative carpets and kilims.

Timney Fowler Design Studio
29 Warple Way, London W3 0RF
Tel. 0181 743 6087 Fax 0181 743 4950
Fabric and wallpaper design, but carpets can be commissioned.

Christine Vanderhurd (see also United States) 2/17 Chelsea Harbour Design Centre, Chelsea Harbour, London SW10 0XE Tel. 0171 351 6332 Fax 0171 376 3574
Contemporary rugs; all designs available in custom sizes, shapes, colours and finishes.

Veedon Fleece
42 Nightingale Road, Guildford, Surrey GU1 1EP Tel./Fax 01483 575 758
A small selection of hand-made high quality modern rugs in both traditional and contemporary designs. Mail order available.

Ian Walker, Odiham Gallery,
78 High Street, Odiham, Hants RG29 1LN
Tel. 01256 703415 Fax 01256 704548
Mainly antique oriental and European carpets.

Gallery Yacou
127 Fulham Road, London SW3 6RT
Tel. 0171 584 2929 Antique oriental carpets.

Helen Yardley
A-Z Studios, 3–5 Hardwidge Street, London SE1 3SY Tel. 0171 403 7114 Fax 0171 407 7520 Contemporary designer rugs.

Karel Weijand
Lion & Lamb Courtyard, Farnham, Surrey
Tel. 01252 726215 Antique and decorative oriental and European carpets.

Zagros Nomadic Carpets & Rugs
Oriental Carpet Centre, 105 Eade Road, London N4 1TJ Tel 0181 800 4001
Fax 0181 800 4002 Oriental tribal carpets.

Specialist Cleaners:

Lannowe Oriental Textiles
March House, 119 High Street, Marshfield, Wilts SN14 8LT Tel. 01225 891 487
Fax 01225 891 182 Specialise in washing, stretching, restoration, conservation, lining, re-dyeing and photography of many types of antique textiles.

Longevity
28 Liddell Road, London NW6 2EW
Tel. 0171 328 4844
Specialist conservation of antique textiles.

Thames Carpet Cleaners
48–56 Reading Road, Henley-on-Thames, Oxon RG9 1AG Tel. 01491 574676

Iran

Miri Iranian Rugs
Bazar, Rahimiyeh Aval, No. 27, Tehran 11636
Tel. 021 561 31 41/561 31 24
Fax 021 561 33 56/563 75 70
Fine new carpets using natural dyes and hand-spun wool in traditional and original designs. For stockists in Europe and America, contact the above.

Italy

Alberto Levi Gallery
Via San Maurilio 24, Milano 20123
Tel. 39 2 89011553 Fax 39 2 72015118
Antique decorative oriental and European carpets; specialise in Chinese carpets.

Eskenazi & C. Srl (see also Great Britain)
Via Borgonuovo 5, Milano 20121
Tel. 39 2 86464883

Fax 39 2 86465018
Antique rugs and textiles; oriental art.

The Netherlands

Kinebanian
Heiligeweg 35, Amsterdam1012 XN
Tel./Fax 020 626 7019 Antique carpets.
Galerie Bernard
Weteringschans 195, Amsterdam 1017 XE
Tel. 020 620 0959
Antique and contemporary carpets.

United States

Anahita Gallery
P.O. Box 1305, Santa Monica, CA 90406
Tel. 213 455 2310
Asia Minor Carpets
236 Fifth Avenue, New York, NY 10001
Tel. 212 447 9066 Fax 212 447 1879
For Europe and Canada distributors contact above; for a list of US distributors call toll-free 1 888 562 4120.
Contemporary oriental rugs of high quality.
Bolour Inc.
595 Madison Avenue, Suite 301, New York, NY 10022 Tel. 212 752 0222
Fax 212 752 4200 Antique oriental and European carpets and tapestries.
Eliko
102 Madison Avenue, 4th Floor, New York, NY 10016 Tel. 212 725 1600 Fax 212 725 1885 Antique and decorative rugs.
F. J. Hakimian
136 E. 57th Street, New York, NY 10022
Tel. 212 371 6900 Fax 212 753 0277
Antique oriental and European carpets.
Claire Murray
P.O. Box 390, Route 5, Ascutney, Vermont, VT 05030 Tel. 802 674 2710. Contemporary hand-hooked rugs in traditional American style, as well as kits for hooked rugs and needlepoint and many other products.
Nourison
5 Sampson Street, Saddle Brook, New Jersey, NJ 07663
Tel. 201 368 6900 Fax 201 368 0739
Sixteenth- to nineteenth-century designs hand-woven in an antique-look process with a high knot density.
James Opie Oriental Rugs
214 SW Stark Street, Portland, Oregon, OR 97204 Tel. 503 226 0116
Renaissance Carpet & Tapestries, Inc.
200 Lexington Avenue, New York, NY 10016
Tel. 212 696 0080 Fax 212 696 4248
Web site: www.RenaissanceCarpets.com
Aubussons, Savonneries and tapestries.
Salon Moderne
281 Lafayette Street, New York, NY 10012
Tel. 212 219 3439 Fax 212 219 9852
Contemporary designer carpets.
Judy Ross
1 Union Square South, Suite 11U, New York, NY 10003 Tel. 212 842 2607 Fax 212 673 5248 Contemporary rug designer.
Santos Gallery,
521 Southwest Tenth Avenue, Portland, Oregon, OR 97205 Tel. 503 227 6650
Antique and decorative oriental carpets.
Christine Vanderhurd (see also Great Britain) 102 Wooster Street, New York, NY 10012 Tel. 212 343 9070 Fax 212 343 2692
Contemporary rugs; all designs available in custom sizes, shapes, colours and finishes.
Sandra Whitman
361 Oak Street, San Francisco, CA 94102
Tel. 415 861 4477 Antique Chinese carpets.
Woven Legends Inc.
4700 Wissahickon Avenue No. 106, Philadelphia, PA 19144 Tel. 215 849 8344
Fax 215 849 8354 For US and European stockists, contact above.
Antique oriental carpets, contemporary carpets and flatweaves.

public collections

The following museums all have noteworthy carpet collections. It is advisable for visitors to contact museums in advance to find out what is on display.

North America
Museum of Fine Art, Boston
The Chicago Art Insititute
The Cleveland Museum of Art
The Henry Ford Museum, Deerborn, Michigan (American rugs)
The Detroit Institute of Art
The Los Angeles County Museum of Art
The Hispanic Society of America, New York (Spanish carpets)
The Metropolitan Museum of Art, New York
The American Museum of Natural History, New York (Navajo rugs and blankets)
The Philadelphia Museum of Art
The Museum of Navajo Ceremonial Art, Santa Fe (Navajo rugs and blankets)
The Textile Museum, Washington DC
The Henry Francis du Pont Winterthur Museum, Delaware (American and English floor coverings)
Canada
The Royal Ontario Museum, Toronto
Austria
Österreichisches Museum für Angewandte Kunst, Vienna
Museum of Ethnology, Vienna
France
Musée Historique des Tissus, Lyon
Musée des Arts Décoratifs, Paris
Mobilier National, Paris (mainly Savonnerie carpets)
Musée du Louvre, Paris
Germany
Museum of Islamic Art, Dahlem, Berlin
Pergamon Museum, Berlin (Islamic collection)
Great Britain
The Burrell Collection, Glasgow
The National Museum of Scotland, Edinburgh (mainly twentieth century)
Victoria & Albert Museum, London
The Whitworth Art Gallery, Manchester
Hungary
Iparmüvészeti Múzeum, Budapest
Italy
Poldi Pezzoli Museum, Milan
Poland
The Sahakian Collection, The Royal Castle, Warsaw (mainly Caucasian)
Turkey
Museum of Turkish and Islamic Art, Istanbul

acknowledgements & credits

Special thanks to Jennifer Wearden of the Victoria & Albert Museum for all her help and advice, and also to my agent Caroline Davidson. I am also most grateful to the following people for assistance with this book: Victoria Harley; Christopher Farr; Karen Howes; Annabel Freyberg; Mary Wondrausch; Nadine Bazar; Mary-Jane Gibson; Mike Tighe; Mary Scott; Laya Patel; Laura Church; Clive Wainwright of the Victoria & Albert Museum; Peter Day, Keeper of Collections, Chatsworth; Bill Irvine and Carolyn Sollis of 'House Beautiful' (USA); Derek Owen and Michael Hawes at David Black's; Alice Richards; Katrin Cargill; Selina Blow; Crispin and Caroline de Moubray; James and Caroline Knox; Lady Victoria Waymouth; Nick Purdon, Ben Evans and Rachel Evans at Hali; Leon Sasson at C. John; Adam Chadwick and Karen Dobbin of Christie's; Marcus Linell and Philippe Garner of Sotheby's; Sue Timney at Timney Fowler; Alison Spear; Jan Baldwin; Sir Tatton Sykes; Christopher Simon Sykes; John Hall; Emma Burns of Colefax & Fowler; Sarah Elson; Norman Bachop; John Eskenazi for help with captions and pictures; and finally my husband, Richard Oldfield.

The publisher thanks the photographers, owners and organisations for their kind permission to reproduce following illustrations in this book.

1 Salon Moderne/John Hall/Judy Ross; **2** Private Collection/National Trust/Geoffrey Shakerley; **4/5** David Black; **8–9** Agence Top/Pascal Hinous/designer Jacques Garcia /Hotel Mansart; **12–13** Elizabeth Whiting & Associates/Rodney Hyett; **15** Museo Thyssen Bornemisza, Madrid; **16** Private Collection/National Trust/Geoffrey Shakerley; **17** Bridgeman Art Library/Christie's Images; **18** Institute of Fine Arts, New York University; **19** Edimedia/ Connaissance des Arts/Pascal Hinous; **20–21** The Interior Archive/Christopher Simon Sykes/Chatsworth House; **22** Museum of Fine Arts Boston/Gift of Mary Louisa Boit, Julia Overing Boit, Jane Hubbard Boit & Florence D. Boit in memory of their father, Edward Darley Boit; **24** Christie's Images; **25** Christie's Images; **27** Jason Shenai/David Black; **28** Roger Viollet; **29** Sotheby's, London; **30–31** Hermitage Museum/Bridgeman Art Library; **33** Marie Claire Maison/Gilles de Chabaneix/Rosensztroch/Suzanne Slesin; **34–35** Christopher Simon Sykes; **36 left** Inside/Côté Ouest/Christoph Dugied/Grand Hotel des Bains – Locquirec; **36–37** The Interior Archive/James Mortimer/designer Jacques Granges; **38 above left** The Interior Archive/Simon Brown/designer John Stefanidis; **38 above right** Christopher Simon Sykes; **38 below** Christopher Simon Sykes; **39** Agence Top/Roland Beaufre/Alexandre Biaggi/designer Jean-Louis Riccardi; **40–41** Agence Top/Roland Beaufre/designer Marroun Salloun; **42–43** Christopher Simon Sykes; **43** Alison Spear/ Sagaponack Farmhouse/carpet designed by Judy Ross for Salon Moderne/dining room chairs by Alison Spear; **44–45** Andrew Wood; **46 above** Paul Ryan/ International Interiors/Jennifer Houser; **46 below** The Interior Archive/Woloszynski; **47** Andrew Wood; **48** The Interior Archive/Fritz von der Schulenburg; **49** Deidi von Schaewen/owner Lillian Williams, Normandy; **50–51** Jean-Pierre Godeaut; **51 above** Robert Harding Picture Library/Joanne Cowie/© IPC Magazines/Country Homes & Interiors; **51 below** The Interior Archive/Woloszynski; **52** John Hall; **53** Jean-Pierre Godeaut; **55–56** Ianthe Ruthven; **56–57** Ianthe Ruthven/Charleston; **58 above** Christian Sarramon/Chateau Balthus; **58 below** Marie Claire Maison/Jean-Pierre Godeaut/Catherine Ardouin; **59–60** National Trust Photo Library/Eric Crichton; **60–63** Christopher Simon Sykes; **64** Inside/Solvi dos Santos; **65** Lars Hallen; **66–67** Inside/Dirand; **68 above** Guy Bouchet; **68 below** Roger Oates Design; **69** Robert Harding Picture Library/Simon Upton/© IPC Magazines/Homes & Gardens; **70–71** Paul Ryan/International Interiors/Ivan Chermayeff; **73** Christian Sarramon/Van Loon; **74 above** The Interior Archive/Christopher Simon Sykes; **74 below** The Interior Archive/Christopher Simon Sykes/reproduced by kind permission of the Earl & Countess of Harewood & the Trustees for the Harewood House Trust; **74–75** The Interior Archive/ Fritz von der Schulenburg; **76–77** Christopher Simon Sykes; **78–79** Paul Ryan/International Interior; **79** Paul Ryan/International Interiors/designers John Saladino & Sharon Casdin; **80 above** Ianthe Ruthven/Leighton House; **80 below** The Interior Archive/Brian Harrison; **81** Agence Top/Pascal Chevallier/Lambert & La Croix; **82 above** Guy Bouchet; **82 below** The Interior Archive/Fritz von der Schulenburg; **82–83** Elizabeth Whiting & Associates/Andreas von Einsiedel/designer Chester Jones; **84** Lars Hallen/ Tureholm Castle, Sweden; **84–85** Ianthe Ruthven/ Leighton House; **86** The Interior Archive/Fritz von der Schulenburg; **87** John Hall; **88 above** The Interior Archive/Fritz von der Schulenburg; **88 below** Guy Bouchet; **89** The Interior Archive/Christopher Simon Sykes; **91** Christian Sarramon/Maison Constant; **92 left** Roger Oates Design; **92–93** Angelo Hornak; **93 right** Andrew Garn; **94–95** Angelo Hornak; **95 right** Christopher Simon Sykes/June Ducas; **96** Jerome Darblay; **97** Christopher Simon Sykes; **98–99** The Interior Archive/Fritz von der Schulenburg; **100** The Interior Archive/Fritz von der Schulenburg; **101** Robert Harding Picture Library/Ianthe Ruthven/© IPC Magazines/ Country Homes & Interiors; **103** The Interior Archive/Woloszynski; **104–105** The Interior Archive/Woloszynski; **105 above** Michael Freeman; **105 below** The Interior Archive/Woloszynski; **106–107** Ianthe Ruthven/Pip Rau; **108 above** Agence Top/Pascal Chevallier/Meerlust property of Hannes Myburg in South Africa; **108 below** Christian Sarramon/B Lippens; **109** Jerome Darblay; **110** Ianthe Ruthven/Pip Rau; **111** Elizabeth Whiting & Associates; **112** Michael Freeman/Rancho de las Golondrinas, Sante Fe; **113** Michael Freeman/Martinez Hacienda; **114–115** Inside/J. P. Largarde; **116–117** Ianthe Ruthven/architect Rolf Blaktad; **118–119** Deidi von Schaewen/Mr & Mrs Levy, Marrakesh; **120** The Interior Archive/Tim Beddow; **121** Deidi von Schaewen/Mr & Mrs Levy, Marrakesh; **123** Helen Yardley (Matt Collection); **124–125** Agence Top/Pascal Chevallier/boathouse of Jean-Jacques Beaume in Neuilly; **126–127** Paul Ryan/International Interiors/Marie France St Felix; **127 right** The Interior Archive/Fritz von der Schulenburg; **128–129** Paul Ryan/International Interiors/ K. Moskal & K. Foreman; **129** Agence Top/Pascal Chevallier/Myrene de Premonville; **130–131** Christopher Simon Sykes/Sarah Elson; **133–134** John Hall/Judy Ross; **135** Agence Top/Pascal a/Chateau de Bagatelle; **136–137** Guy Bouchet; **138** John Sims/Villa, Reale, Lecca; **138–139** Graham Livingstone's warehouse conversion, East London by architect Proctor Matthews/photographed by Nicholas Kane; **140–141** Jean-Pierre Godeaut; **143** Bridgeman Art Library/Christie's Images; **144**, **147**, **152** David Black; **154** Liberty/ Eileen Tweedie; **155**, **156** C. John (Rare Rugs); **157**, **158**, **159**, **160** David Black; **161 left** C. John (Rare Rugs); **161 right** Miri Corp; **162 above** David Black; **162 below** C. John (Rare Rugs); **163**, **164**, **165**, **166** David Black; **167** Clive Loveless; **168**, **169**, **170**, **171**, **172**, **173**, **175**, **176**, **177**, **178**, **179**, **181**, **182**, **183**, **184**, **185**, **186**, **187**, **188**, **189** David Black; **191 left** C. John (Rare Rugs); **191 right** David Black; **192 above** C. John (Rare Rugs); **192 below**, **193** Alberto Levi; **194** C. John (Rare Rugs); **195**, **196 above** Kennedy Carpets/Angelo Hornak; **196 below** C. John (Rare Rugs); **197** Alberto Levi; **199**, **200** C. John (Rare Rugs); **201** Alberto Levi; **202**, **203** C. John (Rare Rugs); **204**, **205** David Black; **206** American Museum of Bath; **207** Mark Fiennes; **208 above** Christie's Images, New York; **208 below** Christie's Images; **209** Sotheby's, London; **210 above** & **middle** Helen Yardley/A/Z Studios; **210 below** Salon Moderne/John Hall/Judy Ross; **211 above** & **middle** Veedon Fleece; **211 below** Sandy Jones/Longevity; **212 above left** & **middle right** Christopher Farr/Georgina von Etzdorf/Longevity; **212 above right** Christopher Farr/Longevity; **212 below right** & **left** Christine Vandurhurd; **213** Nordic Style/Angelo Hornak; **214** Claire Murray; **215** Woven Legends.

index

Numbers in italic refer to pages with illustrations